Dear Debby,
Thank you for your love, support and friendship. Love you! Kathy

In gratitude...
In love...
In yoga...
Kathy Nottis

GOING BEYOND THE POSE

Using Yoga as a Compass to Orient Your Life Toward Happiness

Kathleen Nitting

BALBOA PRESS
A DIVISION OF HAY HOUSE

Copyright © 2018 Kathleen Nitting.

All rights reserved. No part of this book may be used or reproduced by any means, graphic, electronic, or mechanical, including photocopying, recording, taping or by any information storage retrieval system without the written permission of the author except in the case of brief quotations embodied in critical articles and reviews.

Scripture taken from the King James Version of the Bible.

Balboa Press books may be ordered through booksellers or by contacting:

Balboa Press
A Division of Hay House
1663 Liberty Drive
Bloomington, IN 47403
www.balboapress.com
1 (877) 407-4847

Because of the dynamic nature of the Internet, any web addresses or links contained in this book may have changed since publication and may no longer be valid. The views expressed in this work are solely those of the author and do not necessarily reflect the views of the publisher, and the publisher hereby disclaims any responsibility for them.

The author of this book does not dispense medical advice or prescribe the use of any technique as a form of treatment for physical, emotional, or medical problems without the advice of a physician, either directly or indirectly. The intent of the author is only to offer information of a general nature to help you in your quest for emotional and spiritual well-being. In the event you use any of the information in this book for yourself, which is your constitutional right, the author and the publisher assume no responsibility for your actions.

Any people depicted in stock imagery provided by Getty Images are models, and such images are being used for illustrative purposes only. Certain stock imagery © Getty Images.

Print information available on the last page.

ISBN: 978-1-5043-9994-4 (sc)
ISBN: 978-1-5043-9996-8 (hc)
ISBN: 978-1-5043-9995-1 (e)

Library of Congress Control Number: 2018902944

Balboa Press rev. date: 03/27/2018

This book is dedicated to the angels in my life. Your divine inspiration gives voice to my message.

I AM THAT
by Kathleen Nitting

I feel like I'm about to burst open.
I'm looking for space.
Nesting, gestating, I feel the impatience of what's to come.
Glory bubbles inside.
On the wings of a bird, I free fall into the unknown.
No fear.
No regrets.
Only truth.
I burst forth with wild abandon.
I am free.
It is my destiny.
I listen to the sacred.
I marvel at the holy.
Inner truth so strong, it pulls me forward.
I slip back.
I stumble.
I surrender.
I get up.
I rebound.
The inner howl vibrates out beyond,
hauntingly louder and louder.
I am silent.
I listen and I hear.
I breathe it in.
It is life.
It is all there is.
Existence.
I connect to the pulse of it.
I am one with it.
I am that.

Acknowledgements

Thank you to all those who contributed their powerful personal stories to this book. What you've shared helps to illustrate the true meaning of yoga. To my mom, Diane, Rhonda, Robert, Johanna, Diana, Bob, and Themba too, I am grateful.

Thank you, Joanne Delmonico, for sharing your artistry and creating a beautiful mandala as part of the cover art for my book.

A special thank you to Roger Gabriel for serving as an advisor. I am grateful for your generosity in sharing your wisdom, your stories, your humor, and your friendship. You inspired me to delve deeper into The Vedas, while challenging and nourishing the curiosity of my Pitta mind.

To my friends, colleagues and fellow instructors at The Chopra Center, it is an honor to be part of such a special global community. Thank you to the amazing teachers along my yoga journey, particularly Meret whose bright light at every class in Cape Town shaped my own practice and teaching style.

Thank you to Drs. Deepak Chopra and David Simon for their vision to bring the timeless wisdom of yoga, meditation and Ayurveda into the modern world.

To my family and friends, thank you for your love and support. I love you all.

And, finally, I write a special note of honor for my parents. My father was the epitome of truth, courage and integrity, a yogi in his own right. For my mother, whose love and devotion for her family is unwavering, thank you. My love for you is beyond measurement.

Contents

Introduction xi

Chapter 1: Yoga as My Compass 1
Chapter 2: Four Paths of Yoga 8
        i. Bhakti (Love and Devotion) 10
        ii. Jnana (Knowledge) 20
        iii. Karma (Action) 22
        iv. Raja Yoga: the Royal Path (Meditation) 32
            a. Eight Limbs of Yoga 39
Chapter 3: Nature's Intelligence 47
Chapter 4: Meditation and the Gift of Silence 55
Chapter 5: Truth and Authenticity 83
Chapter 6: Living a Conscious Life with Expanded Awareness 104
Chapter 7: God and Yoga 132
Chapter 8: Is Your Compass Off Kilter? 146

References 153

Introduction

Going Beyond the Pose explores the four paths of yoga: *jyana* (knowledge), *bhakti* (love), *karma* (action), and *raja* (meditation) as they are integrated into my life and the lives of interviewees, along with great sages who illustrated and taught the same qualities. The four paths of yoga are presented in ways that are accessible and also experiential and practical, using the guidance of contemporary spiritual leaders; wisdom from notable sages who have left this physical realm; personal stories of my own yogic path; and poignant stories that touched my heart as demonstrations of what it means to be in yoga. Cited are teachings from sacred texts such as the *Upanishads*, *The Yoga Sutras of Patanjali*, the *Bhagavad Gita*, the *Dhammapada*, *Tao de Ching*, and the Bible. A deeper understanding of the philosophy and science of yoga comes from great teachers such as Swami Vivekananda, Paramahansa Yogananda, Jesus, Buddha, Gandhi, and others. Go beyond the pose and discover which of the four paths of yoga naturally resonates with you.

> The broad sympathies and discerning insight needed for the healing of earthly woes cannot flow from mere intellectual consideration of human diversities, but from knowledge of men's deepest unity—kinship with God. Toward realization

of the world's highest ideal—peace through brotherhood—may yoga, the science of personal communion with the divine, spread in time to all men in all lands. (Paramahansa Yogananda)

While studying the history of the ancient Vedas, I fell in love with the deeper essence of yoga, which is within all of us. The idea for the book came about when I began to understand how all the facets of yoga were benefitting me on a profound personal level as the practices were integrated into my daily life, beyond the asanas (yoga poses) and the mechanics of those poses on the yoga mat. Along with glimpses into my own journey are compelling stories that illustrate the principles of yoga. Woven throughout the book are inspirational quotes from sages, scholars, and teachers from all walks of life, offering insight, guidance, and an opportunity to discover, from within, an expanded level of awareness. *Going Beyond the Pose* offers a practical guide to understanding the core principles of living a yogic lifestyle, on and off the mat and outside of any religious implications.

The collection of these real-life, personal experiences I share comes from my own life, along with others from generous souls willing to contribute. As I conducted research for this book, I came upon present-day writings with similar threads of wisdom from ancient texts to help me craft practical tips and tools to gain a greater, more in-depth understanding of the science of yoga as it relates to our contemporary world. What I discovered is that this ancient knowledge is just as relevant today as it was thousands of years ago, and it is really about common sense, accountability, and an intention to connect with and live by universal and natural law. For example, if you want more love in your life, be more loving, and that includes being more loving and compassionate with yourself. If you want peace in the world, be more peaceful in your own world. Give that which you desire to receive.

Author Mark Nepo writes in *The Book of Awakening,* "Certainly true compassion begins with the consideration of others, but the displeasure of others is no reason to muffle your love." So, while my choices of spirituality and yoga may ruffle some feathers, I write from my own experience, and it is one of truth, discovery, exploration, love, and knowing. It is from a place of love that I hope my words are received.

As Swami Paramahansa Yogananda says, "Yoga requires no formal allegiance ... Because the yogic science satisfies a universal need, it has a natural universal appeal."

> There are a number of great men, living today in American or European or other non-Hindu bodies, who, though they may never have heard the words *yogi* or *swami*, are yet true exemplars of those terms. Through their disinterested service to mankind, or through their mastery over passions and thoughts, or through their single-hearted love of God, or through their great powers of concentration, they are, in a sense, yogis; they set themselves the goal of yoga —self-control. These men could rise to even greater heights if they were taught the science of yoga which makes possible a more conscious direction of one's mind and life. Yoga has been superficially misunderstood by certain Western writers, but its critics have never been its practitioners. (Paramahansa Yogananda in *Autobiography of a Yogi*)

In the midst of advancing my studies of the deeper philosophy of yoga a few years ago, I wrote down a book idea that came from wanting to share yoga. I wanted to write about it in such a way as to bring a contemporary understanding to a science that has endured for thousands of years in other cultures. As I read *Autobiography of a Yogi* as research for my manuscript, I made note of how the great

Swami Paramahansa Yogananda's words, written back in 1946, summed up my concept for this book in a few short sentences: "Surely the Yogavatar reached the zenith of all wonders in reducing the ancient complexities of yoga to an effective simplicity within the ordinary grasp."

Psychiatrist and psychologist Dr. Carl Jung is quoted in Yogananda's book for his view about how yoga fulfills not only our needs as humans to seek out spiritual fulfillment but also the "scientific need for facts." Jung, in a speech to the Indian Science Congress in 1937, said, "By reason of its breadth and depth, its venerable age, its doctrine and method, which include every phase of life, it promises undreamed of possibilities … It combines the bodily and the spiritual in an extraordinarily complete way."

The exercises in each chapter entitled "Living Yoga" gently guide you toward shining light on how, in your thoughts, words, and actions, you may already be, without even knowing it as such, in *yoga*, in union with God, the divine source, or universal law. Whatever word or language resonates with you is the perfect way to describe your journey of waking up with an expanded level of consciousness and recognizing your divine nature—that you are a child of God and that you are a sacred part of creation. My hope is that you see even one small spark of your divinity by asking yourself if you come from a place of love in all you do, all you say, all you think. Without judgment or criticism, this kind of self-reflection leads to a more important question: If not, how can I? With each breath of life, we get the opportunity to navigate our lives in the direction of yoga and ultimately toward true happiness.

My goal here is to illustrate, identify, and de-mystify yoga. How can we use the science of yoga to truly reach freedom by liberating ourselves from suffering? Non-attachment is the key. Operate from the heart; always direct the inquiry inward; and challenge your own ego with less need or desire for external approval, affection, appreciation, and attention. Serve yourself through service with and for other sentient beings. With that new level of consciousness comes elevated awareness and conscious choice making. We watch "bad" habits naturally fall away and heart-based ones arise through love, kindness, generosity, laughter, and harmony. Spontaneous right action emerges as a result of a path toward self-realization, and we realize the fulfillment of our truest desires.

Dr. Deepak Chopra tells of an exercise to help rid yourself of an addiction. Each time you want to reach for your vice, whether it is nicotine, alcohol, drugs, or some other addictive behavior, take a moment to become aware of the choice you are making from a heart-centered space, and without judgment, say to yourself, "This is the healthiest choice for me." In many cases, the appetite for that vice diminishes, and you make better choices for the health of your mind, body, and spirit. This is not done easily by just being cynical and ingesting with an attitude of, "Yeah, let's see if this works."

It is an innate awareness that will override the ego's loud distraction if you are willing to commit to yoga practices such as *dhyana* (meditation), *asana* (yoga poses), and *pranayama* (conscious breath work). Throughout the book, the exercises in "Living Yoga" are meant to guide you toward raising self-awareness. Again, it's called a practice, so be easy with yourself in making yoga a daily habit, just like brushing your teeth. If you only ever make a commitment to wake each day with a practice of gratitude, you cannot help but notice the positive effects it will have on your experience in this life.

My intention is to reach people at the soul level, to awaken the universal truth, to continue to expand my own consciousness, and to help you remember that these experiences are always available to you as well. And all of the experiences listed here are available to us for free.

- Develop a meaningful spiritual practice.
- Meditate.
- Practice yoga.
- Pray.

- Spend time in nature.
- Listen to some good music and sing out loud.
- Spend a few moments looking into the eyes of a newborn baby or your pet.
- Pay attention to your body when you laugh or dance with wild abandon.
- Practice gratitude daily. Be mindful of at least one thing for which you are grateful.
- Practice self-care. Replenish, restore, update, download, install new apps, etc. We do this all the time with our electronic devices, but we neglect our greatest device: ourselves and our bodies. Nourish your mind, your spirit, your heart, your physical body, your environment, and your human connections.
- Practice forgiveness.

ONE

YOGA AS MY COMPASS

I'll share with you how one four-letter word led to my undoing. This was not an undoing of my out-of-control, raging ego, but it was the excavation of the human condition as I knew it to be to uncover who I really am. This new awareness led to the unveiling of my pristine soul that gave me the courage to seek out the truth, choose emotional integrity, and honor my true self. That four-letter word is *yoga*.

"The external teacher offers only the suggestion, which arouses the internal teacher." Here, celebrated spiritual leader and monk Swami Vivekananda speaks to direct experience. Whether I am practicing the physical movement in yoga, in search of understanding a particular concept, or examining my own choices and actions, I know that because of the nature of ego, I continually orient my internal compass, finding insight and truth from the internal, eternal source of my soul.

Years ago, I wasn't as prepared for life's curves and twists, literally and figuratively. I know this because in looking back, I see the times where I was inflexible or constricted, played the blame game, sat in the victim's chair, full of disappointment and despair, and used a very different four-letter word. Regret is a waste of precious time. Isn't it really just our thoughts in the form of judgment meant to punish ourselves? I am the first one to admit that those highly charged, reactive (and many times over-reactive) moments weren't pretty at all, definitely not yoga in any form. However, they turned out to be pivotal lessons that would change the trajectory of my life and contribute to my spiritual journey.

So how do we stop the cycle? How do we brave the truth and accept what might come as a result of recognizing our authentic self? In writing this book, I knew I'd have to accept the fallout that would come from those who might reject, condemn, and object. But those who would criticize without any true understanding of yoga aren't my audience anyway. My purpose for writing this book is to express my love and gratitude for the deeper teachings of the ancient wisdom of yoga and teach those who also want to expand their own self-awareness.

The joy of writing this book has come from my internal need, excitement, and passion to share my experience of yoga. When I speak of yoga, I mean going beyond the pose—hence the title of the book—to a deeper understanding of a life philosophy.

When the idea for this book came to me, my intention was to write, motivated by love and truth. I love to write. I always have. So my words are written with love. I ask for divine guidance in communicating my message as the ego easily wants to ask, "What makes you the authority?" The truth is that I fell in love with yoga. I pursued my training in all its disciplines with fervor. I may not be the best or most experienced instructor, but I teach from a place of love. I may not be a scholar about the subjects I write, but the experiences I share are told with integrity. I share experiences of searching for my true self and a deeper meaning for my life in a way that proves to inspire my readers to investigate, explore, excavate, and go beyond the pose and see how yoga can also be a compass for them to create a fulfilling life of perfect health in all areas.

My book is not meant to incite a religious debate, although I suspect some may find certain topics controversial. In writing this book, I was also searching for my expression of transformation—how yoga, the science of yoga, as the title states—beyond the pose, deeply resonated within me. It was instantly familiar. It validated long-suppressed views that felt comfortable in my heart. It brought a fresh breath of excitement and peace for possibilities for a fulfilled life. It wasn't so much discovering my truth as it was this sensation of remembering it, as if I cracked a shell around me and felt safe and supported, despite the risk. I also felt vulnerable, alone, and lost while I volleyed between what I thought my reality to be and the truth as I now saw it. As Buddha said, "It is our destiny as human beings to make this journey ourselves." There is no deliberate doctrine or mandate here, but a slight nudge, a gentle suggestion to look in the mirror for yourself, at yourself, within yourself.

These days, using yoga to guide me toward acceptance, letting go, healing, and moving on—both on and off the mat—and now, when possible, I respectfully opt out of potentially volatile conversations, or avoid situations altogether that may not honor me, not the ego me, but God's version of me. On the mat, when doing my yoga class, I use my body as an internal compass and follow that, not comparing myself to others or worrying whether they are doing the same. In this way, I avoid injury and self-criticism and really enjoy how my body feels during and after a yoga class like this. I do admit that I still glance over to admire those students who effortlessly make their way into a full expression of headstand. And I fondly remember, prior to my back surgery, how I was unable to attempt *bakasana* or crow pose. Instead, I would challenge myself by encouraging and directing my fellow classmate successfully into the pose. In a dynamic exchange of giving and receiving, we both experienced the reward of having conquered the pose. For me, I felt elated to see my friend accomplish the feat, while my confidence grew as an effective yoga instructor. For Sara, strength, balance, flexibility, and her own sense of confidence emerged. For me, this experience saw blurred lines between teacher and student as I learned as much as I taught that day.

Yoga teaches us that flexibility, endurance, and strength come with detachment from the outcome, whether it's trying to achieve a particular asana in class or navigating daily life. The physical benefits of yoga go way beyond the pose. I have personally felt stronger, leaner, and more flexible. I am also more centered, leaner in my material desires, and more flexible in my attitudes. I may not be the best teacher out there, but I am authentic in my love for the practice of yoga. I am not yet able to twist myself up like a pretzel or hold my own body weight upside down with one palm, but I am conscious of my breath, and I honor my body, mind, and spirit from wherever I may be in that particular moment. And I guide my students to the do the same.

The first words that come to mind when I think of the meaning of yoga are calm, strength, flexibility, balance, and wellbeing. To me, yoga represents a path to perfect health in mind, body, and spirit. It means practicing awareness and centeredness in thoughts, words, and actions. It means transformation from an ego-based consciousness or object referral to one of a higher level of consciousness or self-referral. My own definition of yoga has evolved over the years, where it has gone from being the right exercises for my back injury and weight management to my special place where I take time and care for myself. With the study of the ancient wisdom found in the Vedic texts, written more than five thousand years ago, my definition has now evolved to a greater understanding of yoga. It has become my life's compass, as I look to the philosophy of yoga as a guide to living in the fullness of my true nature with balance and equanimity.

Swami Vivekananda describes what it means to be in yoga, in union, to be yoked. "When a person has reached the highest state of Unity, seeing neither man nor woman, neither sect nor creed, nor color, nor birth, nor any of these differentiations, but goes beyond and finds that One Infinite Spirit behind every human being—only then has that person reached the universal brotherhood." The word *communion* means to be "in union." Enthusiasm means *en theos* or "in spirit." We all know one experience or another that has brought us to our knees, taken our breath away, left us speechless, or left us feeling like we've reached a religious epiphany. All of these expressions describe the essence of yoga, that indescribable feeling of awe, wonder, and connection, beyond human thinking, where the spirit, the soul, the true essence of who you really are gets to shine forth in front of the ego, even if for only a brief moment. If you can remember that inexpressible feeling, then you accessed yourself at the soul level. Through yoga, our self-awareness is expanded, allowing this pure bliss to infiltrate all areas of our lives. One of my teachers says that even meditating once will have a positive influence on your life and the lives of those around you.

Before delving into the study of yoga, there were already ways I was practicing without knowing it as yoga. Since I was a child, I knew I had a passion for the written word. Time and space would dissolve as I was absorbed in a good book. Back then, I'd sit for hours reading the liner notes of albums from my favorite rock stars in deep appreciation for the cleverly crafted lyrics. Or I'd sit with a yellow legal pad and pencil composing my own prose or poetry. And I still lose time in the words of a well-written song or an eloquently constructed paragraph of a favorite author. Each time I feel that kind of connection with the essence of who I really am, I feel united in a profound way. That is to be in yoga. To stand in the face of adversity and still honor myself could only leave me feeling a sense of connectedness with a deeper truth. To live in alignment with one's true purpose is to be in yoga.

It is written in *The Yoga Sutras of Patanjali,* "The mind becomes clear and serene when the qualities of the heart are cultivated." Imagine, if you can, a world where everyone gets to live their true purpose, to fulfill their dreams, to live a life as their authentic selves without the worry of criticism, condemnation, or control. There would be an ease with which we would live in accord with each other, trusting that God would provide. Sutra 1.13 states, "The practice of yoga is the commitment to become established in the state of freedom." We can only be truly free through self-study, self-inquiry, and self-acceptance. From this heart-centered place, we are then open to accept others as they are too.

The miracles, the lessons, the teachers, the whispers, the screams, the opportunities—they are always there for us, even when we aren't paying attention. But when we do pay attention to our self, we see God everywhere. Synchronicity, coincidences, unexpected surprises, questions, and answers become normal, and you begin to realize the abundance of this divine universe. You become just like Neo decoding your own matrix and becoming witness to your suffering falling away. Please notice that I did not say your life becomes a piece of cake, where there is no sadness or there are no challenges. As author and spiritual leader Wayne Dyer said in his book *Change your Thoughts—Change your Life*, "When you change the way you look at things, the things you look at change."

Living Yoga

Throughout the book, *Living Yoga* offers you the opportunity to put yoga philosophy into practice in your own life. Here is an exercise in perception. Think of a time when something unpleasant happened. What were the facts? Did you judge the situation as good or bad? Was your perception truth, or did it just seem true for you in that moment? In retrospect, were there other details you chose not to see? As an exercise in compassion, ask yourself if you would be willing to see the other person's point of view. This doesn't mean to condone a harmful behavior but to see from what level of awareness the other person may have been operating. If your behavior caused harm to another, would you be willing to try an exercise in self-love? Without guilt or shame, take responsibility for your actions. Show yourself love by knowing that by moving forward, because you are more aware, you get to make a different choice, from a more expanded state of consciousness. Forgiveness is one of the greatest examples of self-love. Find ways to practice gratitude for these life experiences and the growth that comes from lessons learned.

The next time you find yourself in an uncomfortable situation or something disagreeable happens, see if you can catch yourself in the moment and just observe. What will you choose? How will you respond? This new self-inquiry, self-awareness, and acceptance of what is—this is yoga!

Two

Four Paths of Yoga

Spiritual teacher Swami Vivekananda wrote, "Freedom of the soul is the goal of all yogas ... and each one equally leads to the same result." From the ancient language Sanskrit root *yuj* (pronounced "yug"), yoga means union or reunion with God.

According to the wisdom of ancient scriptures, there are four main paths of yoga, which are classified or aligned according to the differing natures of humankind. The first of these paths is bhakti, the yoga of love and devotion. Karma is the yoga of action, through works of duty or selfless service. Jnana (pronounced Gyan) is the yoga of science and knowledge. Raja or the royal path is yoga through self-discipline and gaining control of one's mind. Raja yoga is referred to as the royal path because it is rich in knowledge and experience. It is inclusive of all the paths, providing a framework to put these life principles, known as the eight limbs of yoga, into practice.

Without even knowing it, many of us may already demonstrate yogic principles in our day-to-day lives. *Going beyond the Pose* looks at how we can integrate more yoga into our daily existence and illustrates how the philosophy of these ancient teachings can complement and enhance our lives without any threat or betrayal of our current belief systems. As individuals, we all come to this world with our own unique personalities, shaped, directed, and often dictated by the many layers of our lives: family, culture, race, creed, socioeconomic standing, and other influences. Recognizing that each of us has our own journey, whether spiritual or not, one or more of the four yogic paths may resonate more easily.

The eight limbs of yoga are a roadmap for an authentic life. Engaging in these practices, you will begin to celebrate a relationship with God that no one other than you can experience. You have your own personality, your own body, your own soul, and your own purpose in this life. By accessing the ancient wisdom of yoga and integrating mind, body, spirit, and your environment, you will be guided by the divine compass that resides within you, and you will discover that you don't have to be taught anything. As Swami Vivekananda states, "Yoga, through which divinity is found within, is doubtless, the highest road."

My teacher and friend Roger Gabriel says, "There's nothing to learn. We are here to remember what we already know; we've just forgotten." The eight limbs of yoga are not rungs on a ladder, where we perfect one step and move on to the next. We don't seek them in a progressive order. Rather, we move through each practice continuously just as we traverse the many layers of our lives all the time, adjusting, expanding, and evolving. And when we've steered off course, we can choose to learn the lesson, and once again, we adjust, expand, and evolve. This is the dance of life.

Beyond the mindfulness practice of observing our breath, meditation goes even deeper into witnessing awareness when we allow our thoughts to come and go just as effortlessly as our breath. Delving deeper, we find inner silence, and we freely gravitate toward the practice of the eight limbs of yoga, while egocentric behaviors naturally fall away. Along the way, I've learned to trust my internal compass, with its foundation in the eight limbs of yoga and discovered what has always been present: strength, courage, and innate wisdom.

Can you follow only one path? Or is each path of yoga the door or window to the next? Can you be in complete devotion to God as with bhakti yoga without being compassionate toward others or yourself, without being self-reflective (raja yoga)? Can you live a life of selfless service (karma yoga) without being in total union with God? Can you not come to truth (jnana yoga) without naturally abiding by the universal laws of nature?

Although the Vedic texts describe four different paths of yoga, they are not mutually exclusive. "In the end, all these four paths converge and become one." In the same way, all religions lead to the same goal. Swami Vivekananda said, "By study of different religions, we find that in essence they are one." It is our intrinsic nature to search for and remember the essence of who we really are. Stripped of the veil of ego and at our core, we are one; we are love; we are yoga.

Vivekananda illustrates so beautifully that attachment to ego and constriction of thought will never bring the true experience of God: "We find that all religions teach the eternity of the soul as well as its luster has been dimmed and that its primitive purity is to be regained by the knowledge of God. It is good to be born in a church, but bad to die there. Ideals and methods may differ, but that is the central point ... There is that beyond all books, beyond all creeds, beyond the vanities of this world and it is the realization of God within yourself."

Bhakti (Love and Devotion)

Swami Vivekananda describes bhakti yoga as the science of higher love. Indian yogi Paramahansa Yogananda says, "Mere intellectual willingness or open-mindedness is not enough. Only adequate enlargement of consciousness by yoga practice and devotional *Bhakti* (love) can prepare one to absorb the liberating shock of omnipresence."

"To be in love with someone or something creates separation. Bhakti is to BE love; to be intoxicated with Divine Love. It is the Unity of being in love with love itself ... It is this deep yearning of our soul for joy and bliss, which eventually re-ignites our search for God. Bhakti is the journey to finally rest in God." In his article *Bhakti Yoga —The Path of Love*, Vedic scholar Roger Gabriel (Raghavanand) eloquently illustrates the yogic path of love and devotion to the divine through the complete surrender of the ego. Love in its purest form is without motive, reward, or worldly acquisitions.

"The Pure Heart is the best mirror for the reflection of the truth." When your intention is heart-centered and coming from a loving place, rather than your intellect, you experience less suffering. Vivekananda, in describing a person who follows bhakti yoga said, "A Bhakta cares for nothing but love, to love and to be loved." At first I thought that this person should not care about being loved. But when applying the principles of the universal law of giving and receiving, the care to be loved is a way of receiving the gift of love, therefore allowing the dynamic exchange of this same energy to remain uninterrupted. Upon further investigation, reading the ancient texts—the Upanishads, the Yoga Sutras of Patanjali, the Dhamapada—it became clear to me that bhakti yoga is about love and devotion to God, yes. But in practicing the bhakti path of yoga here in this physical realm we call life, the deeper meaning is to see God in everyone and everything. The English essence of the beautiful Sanskrit blessing *namaste* is, "The divine light in me recognizes the divine light in you." With your palms together and hands at your heart (also known as prayer position), it is considered a sign of deep respect, love, and gratitude, a soul-to-soul connection acknowledging that, at a deeper level, we are all one. That is the only truth.

Dr. Deepak Chopra says in *The Path to Love*, "Love pulls you out of ego boundaries, and when you are dedicated to acting from love, you are able to live in spirit."

There are people who come into this world never losing their connection to the divine and spend the entirety of their lives in love and devotion to God. Others are inspired by a vision, a near-death experience, or some other out-of-this-realm occurrence that sets them on a path to truly live as a bhakti yogi. Spiritual leader Panache Desai is someone I would consider to be a bhakti yogi, seeing and feeling the presence of God in everyone and everything. There are children who remember their mystic experiences into adulthood. It's quite powerful to see and hear them speak with such conviction of the truth about God. As an adult, Panache Desai rediscovered this truth, which he knew as a small child, and now shares his gifts with others, helping them to remember the truth of who they really are.

The famous artist Akiane Kramarik, featured on *The Oprah Winfrey Show* at the age of eight as a child prodigy, claims she gets the visions for her art from God, and her paintings are truly unworldly in their beauty. Author Mattie Stepanek was riddled with a rare mitochondrial disease, confining him to a wheelchair and subjecting him to brutal medical treatments as a toddler. But as a preteen, this remarkable little boy spoke only of God's love, becoming famous for his books of poems called *Heart Songs*. He wrote with a wisdom far beyond his years, "I have a song, deep in my heart. And only I can hear it. If I close my eyes and sit very still, it is so easy to listen to my song … Everyone in the whole wide world has a special heart song. If you believe in magical, musical hearts, and if you believe you can be happy, then you, too, will hear your heart song." This contemporary sage knew that the real voice of happiness resides in our hearts.

Bhakti yoga is said to be the simplest of paths because one need only make a commitment to see God in everyone and everything. In *The Path to Love*, Deepak Chopra recounts a conversation with a patient who struggled with how she was showing up in her love life. Dr. Chopra asked her to contemplate the following, "Being shown a gesture of love is like being offered a portion of God." When we approach life with this awareness, we practice bhakti yoga. We can extend those gestures of love, and we can appreciate and receive them with the same generosity of spirit. That is to be in yoga.

Bhakti is also the path taken by the ancient mystics of Christianity, Judaism, and Islam, who used prayer, ritual, and devotion to know God. However, Swami Vivekananda reminds us, "So long as we think of God as sitting above the clouds, with a reward in one hand and punishment in the other, there can be no love."

Swami Vivekananda describes the intent of one who practices bhakti yoga to always elevate his emotions toward excellence, moving toward living a life with greater purpose beyond the physical pleasures and pains of our body and ego. "The bhakta says that not one of our feelings is wrong; he takes hold of them all and points them unfailingly toward God."

My dear friend Johanna's devotion to love affords her the capacity to set aside someone's bad behavior and see only divinity. Her all-encompassing love and devotion to God are admirable. Yet even she is faced with trials and tribulations but holds in her awareness that God's love directs her through these dark moments. Family tensions cause her distress. She is saddened by the unkind acts, praying for resolution. In a brave moment, in an effort to break the tension and ease her mother's pain due to the rift among siblings and guided only by her desire to come from a place of love, she asked for forgiveness, despite knowing there was no offense on her part. What else could she do? She could not control the others' behavior. So she chose to accept peace in her heart, knowing she did what her love and devotion for God guided her to do, regardless of the outcome. And while painful, sometimes those rifts cannot be repaired. Mark Nepo writes, "The pain was necessary to know the truth." In her own pain of trying to resolve the conflict, Johanna discovered, in this particular situation, her truth, which is that she did her best. She didn't harm. She didn't gossip, judge, or take revenge. She forgave. The relationship remains strained or maybe even permanently broken, but she forgave, and now she can move on, knowing her heart is cleansed. Her mind is clear of any speculation. Nepo says, "At last, the wound, even if never acknowledged by the other person, can heal, and our life can continue."

Johanna continually asks herself how she can demonstrate her love for God right now, today, in this moment. It is a deep sense of connection demonstrated in her daily rituals, prayer, song, dance, devotion, dedications, community, and selfless service. Even more powerful is her unwavering love and devotion, which result in spontaneous right action. She lives a life of bhakti yoga.

During the Easter weekend, attendance at Johanna's church can reach beyond 9 million parishioners. It's one of the largest gatherings of the year for the ZCC (Zion Christian Church) in South Africa. Members from the church offer their services to sew church uniforms, cook, clean, and a number of other tasks in preparation for the Easter festivities. During the early morning hours, Johanna changed into her work clothes, reserving her favorite corduroy skirt to wear for the holiday services. After the long day of volunteering, Johanna went back to collect her things and noticed that her favorite skirt had been stolen. And although I'm sure she was brokenhearted about it, she told me that in that moment, she asked that all who laid eyes on her skirt would know and receive God's love. I remember thinking how remarkable it was that her first thought was to wish the peace of God's love. She never spoke of it again. She never wished evil upon the thief. In an admirable display of compassion, Johanna said to me, "It's obvious the person needed it more than I." This was one of the many demonstrations by Johanna of what it means to practice bhakti yoga.

In another instance, Johanna and I were discussing the issue of trust between employee and boss, sharing stories we'd heard of housekeepers finding money in their bosses' pockets while doing the laundry. A prevalent attitude was that if the person left that money in the pocket, he or she was rich enough not to miss it. Johanna's response to those situations was, "It doesn't matter whether you see or not. I wouldn't take even one cent of a Rand because God will see." (As a point of reference, the equivalent to that South African currency would be about .001 of a US penny.) Without knowing what bhakti yoga is, Johanna's life is guided by her love and devotion to God.

Here is a story of a mother's love and devotion. After a very long day, working a full-time job as a bookkeeper for her parents' business, my mother did what most women were expected to do back in the early 1960s. She went home, cooked a meal for her family, cleaned the kitchen, and then set off to do the rest of the chores. One of those duties that she would do on this particular night was iron clothes. In those days, there were no steam irons and there were no convenient cans of starch. Instead, my mom made her own boiled starch, out of corn flour. When I remarked about how much work and how messy the whole process was, my mother's reply was typical of the dutiful housewife. She said, "Yes, but the shirts come out so crisp and look so beautiful." As she tells it, my mom stayed up into the early hours of the morning, while her husband, my father, and her young daughter, my eldest sister, slept. Feeling proud of having finished the entire load of ironing, my mom left the neat pile and went to sleep.

When she woke up a few hours later, she could hear that her child was already awake and busy. Exhausted, my mom crawled out of bed to greet my sister and probably prepare her breakfast. She said she nearly collapsed at what she discovered. There in the living room was her little girl with her toy ironing board and iron and the now-wrinkled pile of clothes my mom had worked so hard to finish the night before.

With her eyes beaming with pride and a smile from ear to ear, she said, "Look, Mommy, I ironed the clothes for you."

I could feel the weight of that moment and asked my mother, "What did you do?"

This is where you see bhakti yoga in action. Seeing the pure joy and love in her daughter's eyes, my mother chose absolute devotion to her family in place of her own disappointment and maybe even fury and received her baby's "gift" with the same joy and love in which it was given.

I heard Eckhart Tolle speak about this. He told the story of a woman who was unable to keep her meditation practice going, as much as she tried. Her family took up all of her time. She felt sad, guilty, and defeated. Tolle then explained to her that her loyalty and commitment to her family was very admirable and the work she was doing each and every day was important. Tolle's advice to her was this: Make the devotion to your family your meditation. Don't complain. Be present with each task, no matter how mundane. This is bhakti yoga.

Living Yoga

Set an intention to be present with everything. Thich Nhat Hanh says, "If you are washing the dishes, be present with the activity of washing the dishes rather than complaining about how much you hate doing the dishes; steeping in the irritation or allowing your mind to wander." Maybe it's your day to carpool the children to soccer practice. Be present. Whatever the perceived mundane activity, have the intention to be present, offer it up to God, or simply put your full attention on the task at hand, observing the moment as it is, without judgment, without complaint. In this way, you live in present moment awareness and begin to feel the fullness of life, of your own existence and the connection to all life.

The birth of a child or just staring at a child in wonder can bring most people to that place of pure joy and unconditional love. My friend Eileen recently became a grandmother, and you can hear and see the insurmountable joy as she describes being in the presence of her grandson, not quite ten months old at the time of this particular conversation. I suggested that she journal about her daily experiences with him. Not only has she been journaling of the bliss she feels, but she also writes daily messages for him to read when he is older. A regular meditator, Eileen notices how much her grandson enjoys being in this timeless, boundless space with his grandmother while they meditate together as she whispers to him, "We're resting in existence. We're resting in awareness. We're resting in being." Together, they share yoga.

This next story is one to which many will relate, whether it mirrors your own experience or is the familiar story of someone you know. It is about a caretaker whose selflessness demonstrates yoga in action. Nineteenth-century Indian mystic and yogi Ramakrishna said, "Through selfless work, love of God grows in heart."

One of my dearest friends was present for the recent passing of her mother. In the months leading up to Dotty's death, Rhonda became power of attorney for all of her mom's legal matters and had authority over the medical directive. Without fail or question, my friend oversaw the care and wellbeing of her mom, cleaning, feeding, and carrying her, bringing familiar items for her room to make sure Dotty felt a sense of home while in hospice care. I remember Rhonda saying in her Southern drawl, "I'm going to make sure my momma knows she is loved." My friend's strength and resilience were extraordinary, despite her own physical and emotional pain and suffering. It was a deep and profound experience, and it was raw, but that never stopped her from trying each day to ease her mother's fear and pain. For that, she will have no regrets.

Less than a year later, Rhonda took on the same responsibilities for her father, who was diagnosed with stage 4 stomach cancer. Finding appropriate hospice care, no matter how good, never feels sufficient for our loved ones as we struggle with the tough decisions required for their care. It was an emotional, physical, and financial anvil on her shoulders as my friend commuted back and forth for months between Oregon, California, and Georgia to be with her father. A week after Thanksgiving, I received the message that read, "My daddy passed peacefully." And in a bit of comic relief for both of us, Rhonda butt dialed me with her cell phone, so we talked as she drove the back roads of Georgia to be with her family. I knew she was relieved to know he was no longer in pain, but I could feel the sorrow of the little girl who lost both of her parents in the span of one year. While being their caretaker was difficult and oftentimes inconvenient, the daughter's love and devotion was unquestionable and of the purest form. This is bhakti yoga in action.

What now? My friend is experiencing what most of us have felt at some transitional point in our lives. A feeling of loss, emptiness, and confusion has crept in as she struggles to understand her purpose in life. It is not uncommon for people to experience this type of disorientation following the passing of a loved one or someone for whom they've cared. I remind my friend that in the same way she unconditionally extended love and devotion to her parents, it was now time for her to demonstrate that love and devotion to the person she had been neglecting while her time and attention were redirected. That person is herself. Nourishing and honoring oneself, when authentic, is also a sacred act of love, of bhakti yoga.

The *Bhagavad Gita*, a beautiful poem written as a love song to God, is so revered in India for the intensity of its expression of love. The *Gita* says, "All paths lead to me." Ancient Vedic texts made no reference to one religious path being better than another. This quote, "All paths lead to me," illustrates that in truth, all paths will lead to God.

I remember being in a bookstore when a woman and her child walked in. The little girl's eyes were sparkling with sheer joy and anticipation of having a book read to her. You could tell by the pace of her walk that the mother had a definite destination aisle in the store for which she was heading. A while later, I saw the same little girl trying to get her mom's attention. She started with an excited tone in her voice and a book in her hand, "Mommy … Mommy." But no acknowledgment came. I've done it. I'm sure you can also remember a time too. We seek someone's love, attention, and affection, so we ask; then we ask louder, and even louder we plead in desperation, allowing ourselves to seep in that sense of rejection. The mother and her daughter were very close to where I was sitting, and I became distracted from what I was reading. I became witness to what happened next. The little one pulled on her mother's shirt, pleading, "Mommy ... Mom ... Mommy." Her mom swatted the girl's hand away, telling her to stop and leave her alone. I recognized the defeat in that young girl's eyes, and it tore at my heart strings. If the mom had been present for that split second to extend a loving smile, it would have made all the difference.

This story is a reminder to all of us that we become more aware of how our actions, words, and thoughts can affect others. Babies and young children only live in the moment. Without judgment, maybe even a bit of compassion for the woman, I understood she was under a time constraint. She entered the store already in a rush and probably had many more errands to get done, or maybe the child had been asking for her mom's attention all day. Whatever the case, one glance of love or a smile in validation would have made all the difference for that little girl.

Living Yoga

Smile. Offering a smile to someone often has an impact greater than you will ever know. Maybe the elderly person you smiled at was feeling lonely, but your smile made her feel connected for a moment. Give a silent blessing to someone as he or she passes you on the street. Are you able to give that same blessing to the person who bumped into you without apologizing, or the guy who flipped you a vulgar gesture because you missed the traffic light? When practicing bhakti yoga, love and devotion are non-discriminating. Everyone and everything is seen as a creation of God. Say a prayer for someone or send him or her a silent prayer of gratitude. Make a commitment to be patient with your child who asks why every few seconds.

Bhakti is the path of total surrender and devotion, offering everything to God. For modern/contemporary Western thinking, the bhakti path becomes a state of mind, to find that place within yourself where you experience only love, and ultimately unity with God. Vivekananda taught, "The reward of love is love, and what a reward it is! It is the only thing that takes off all sorrows, the only cup by the drinking of which the illusory sufferings of the world vanish."

JNANA (KNOWLEDGE)

Jnana yoga (pronounced "gyan") is the yoga of right knowledge or true knowledge. The ultimate truth as described by ninth-century Indian philosopher and theologian Adi Shankara in *The Crest Jewel of Discrimination* is that there is no separation between you and me. At the core of the ancient principle of Advaita, or no-dualism, as described by Shankara, is that we are all unique expressions of the same reality. True knowledge is not found in doctrine or dogma but through direct experience, through deep meditation and contemplation.

Adi Shankara was known to have systemized the science of yoga, establishing monasteries and yoga schools throughout India. He was responsible for reviving the ancient Vedanta philosophies and teaching the concept of nondualism. There is no separation. Everything is connected. Through the practice of meditation, we can traverse our perceived realities to higher states of consciousness, where we recognize this truth of inter-connectedness.

Swami Vivekananda wrote, "This is what *Jnana* Yoga teaches. It teaches us that we are divine. It shows to all humanity the real unity of being; that each one of us is a manifestation on earth of the Lord God … all are manifestations of the same God." In another passage, he said, "Thus a tremendous statement is made by all religions that the human mind transcends not only the limitations of the senses, but also the power of reasoning." So, while we might debate one dictate over another, at the soul level, there is a deeper knowing.

Jnana Yogi Sri Nisargadatta Maharaj spoke of this universal theme when he said, "In my world, there is community, insight, love and real quality; the individuality is the totality ... All are one, and the One is all." Walt Whitman expressed this universal truth of non-duality in *Song of Myself*, "For every atom belonging to me as good belongs to you." Don't these familiar sentences illustrate the same thing? "I am not my sister's keeper; I am my sister." "Do unto others as you would have them do unto you." "Love your neighbor as yourself."

Jnana yogi Ramana Maharishi asked the existential question, "Who am I?" The practice of jnana yoga has the truth seeker asking this big question of who am I, along with others, including those I learned and now teach in meditation: What is my purpose? What do I want? For what am I grateful? Is this all there is?

In his book *The Path to Love*, Dr. Deepak Chopra describes jnana as, "the mind in communion with spirit." In a fear-based and scarcity-thinking mind-set, one cannot move beyond the ego's constant threat of loss and lack. In the beautiful words of Persian poet Hafiz, "Fear is the cheapest room in the house. I'd like to see you in better living conditions." With an openness of heart and mind, one can move past the fear. Jnana yoga guides us toward trusting our innate sense of oneness. If one is abundant, we are all abundant.

Deepak Chopra echoes the great sages when he warns of the darker side of the pursuit of spiritual knowledge if we are not diligent in our system of checks and balances with our own ego. He writes in *The Seven Spiritual Laws of Yoga*, "The Yoga of Knowledge can be a wonderful path if we are mature enough to understand that there are seductive temptations that may entrap us for a while in diversions of the intellect." Jnana yoga is referred to as a double-edged sword because the attainment of knowledge toward self-realization can also lead one toward an inflated ego and spiritual pride from believing perceived intellect makes one superior. As with all journeys toward enlightenment, no one path is grander.

I think this may be true for each path of yoga. If we pursue anything for external fame, fortune, or pride, including with a spiritual journey, we will fall prey to our ego's temptations. We read about how Jesus found this to be true on his forty days in the desert. Without self-awareness, self-inquiry, and constant orientation of our compass, even the most enlightened of humans will be tempted to be led astray.

In his poem entitled *Samadhi* (Sanskrit for enlightenment), Vivekananda attempts to convey the indescribable joy and peace that comes with this knowledge of union or yoga. "Smoldering joy, oft-puffed by meditation, blinding my tearful eyes, burst into immortal flames of bliss, consumed by tears, my frame, my all. Thou art I. I am Thou, knowing, knower, known, as One!" When the veil of illusion (*maya* in Sanskrit) vanishes, the universal truth arises.

Living Yoga

How can we put jnana yoga into practice? "Seek the company of those who seek Enlightenment, but run from those who claim to have found it." There have been many renditions of this particular idea, but the gist of this concept is the same. On your own path, remember to question, listen, and learn; but ultimately, find the answers from within.

Karma (Action)

"Through selfless service, you will always be fruitful and find fulfillment of your desires. This is the promise of the Creator." In the *Bhagavad Gita*, Krishna guides Arujuna toward the understanding that any action done for selfish motives will not lead to fulfillment but will only increase these egoistic desires. When our sense of self is wrapped up in obsessions like physical beauty, material wealth, and our own inflated level of importance, our lives lose balance, leading to internal suffering. As Swami Vivekananda explains, "Karma yoga tell us to enjoy all the beauty of the world, but not to identify ourselves with any of it ... Misery comes through attachment to the things of the world, not through work ... Non-attachment is the basis for all yoga ... Freedom of the soul is the goal of all yoga."

The Vedanta Society of California defines karma yoga as the path of dedicated work: renouncing the results of our actions as a spiritual offering rather than hoarding the results for ourselves.

Thirteenth-century theologian, philosopher, and mystic Meister Eckhart said, "What we plant in the soul of contemplation, we shall reap in the harvest of action." Other sacred texts, such as the Bible, say nearly the same. 2 Corinthians 9:6 (KJV) reads, "But this [I say], He which soweth sparingly shall reap also sparingly; and he which soweth bountifully shall reap also bountifully." However, in the contemporary world, there can be a misunderstanding of this concept of cause and effect, action and reaction, choice and consequence. When doing research for this book, I discovered many quotes on the concept of karma that pointed to a "you'll get yours" attitude. Karma is not good or bad; it is not rooted in vengeance; it is not out to get you. All action creates a force of energy that produces a reaction of like kind. This is the essential nature of the universal law of karma. Without any self-awareness, many people see life as happening "to" them. "Did you see that guy deliberately cut me off? Why is this happening?" Many people suffer as they live with attitudes of, "Why me?" or "Poor me." When we are not self-aware and live in victim consciousness, our power to direct life is given over to luck, bad and good; or we buckle down in a defensive stance, reacting rather than consciously taking action.

We can shift our focus away from ourselves, our drama, and our problems and instead, focus on others through acts of love and service. Kindness just for the sake of kindness brings more joy, hope, and fulfillment. Swami Vivekananda says, "Every act of charity, every thought of sympathy, every act of help, every good deed, takes so much self-importance away from our little selves."

Another way is to take a higher approach, not minimizing our stories but taking an active role in transforming them. That is the real choice. While we can't change some of the horrific, terrifying, sad, disappointing, and traumatic events, we get to choose what those life experiences are meant to teach us—how you stepping out of your darkness can provide a hand for someone else to be lifted out of his or her darkness too. It isn't easy, and it can seem impossible or even offensive to hear someone say you should get over it. There have been so many brave people who have shared their stories and given others the courage to do the same. Today we see therapists, life coaches, counselors, and spiritual teachers providing guidance and skillful tools to assist with the healing process. In the words of contemporary spiritual leader and author Iyanla Vanzant, "You've got to do your work." And that's where the choice is. We get to either steep in the stories that often destroy our lives, our relationships, our health, and the quality of this precious life. Or we get to excavate the muck and find a way up and out. That's where the freedom lies.

Author Daniel Coleman writes in his book *Emotional Intelligence*, "There is much to be said for the constructive contribution of suffering to creative and spiritual life; suffering can temper the soul." This is where the real work begins. It's where we make the choice to become the sufferer/the story or we transmute the suffering into seeking and finding the blessing in our darkest hour. I have been very blessed in my life to know that my suffering and my heartbreak doesn't hold a candle to others. I don't say this to diminish my pain or compare stories to see whose is more relevant, more poignant or more tragic. I say I am blessed because I see others' pain and I feel it deeply. I have learned now how not to absorb that pain. It's a constant practice to be empathic without storing someone else's pain in my own physical body and emotional stability. Through selfless service, I can be at peace with how I deal with my own pain as well as help others to relieve some of theirs.

Buddha says, "Fly in the sky, burrow in the ground, you cannot escape the consequences of your actions." I remember a colleague, who I'll call Vince, at the now-defunct Internet startup where I worked many years ago. Initially, Vince received many odd glances and judgments as he had full sleeves, which in tattoo circles means his arms were covered in ink. While working on a project together, I tried to keep myself from also judging him based only on his appearance. I asked about his tattoos, and he proceeded to open up to me about his life. Turns out, Vince was an ex-convict, recovering heroin addict, and former drug dealer. He was more than forthcoming about his "checkered past," as he referred to it. He was in his late teens when he first tried heroin, and very quickly, his life spiraled out of control. He sold drugs to maintain his addiction, and he was eventually arrested and tried as an adult for his drug crimes. But the more interesting part of the story for me was how he got to prison. In desperation for her son's life, his own mother turned him in. Vince told me that what his mother did was the single most important moment of his life. Where most would be enraged by such a betrayal, Vince turned toward love and gratitude, and that made all the difference.

Rather than continue the dark path of drugs, violence, and other criminal activities in prison, Vince was able to rise above his addiction and become a talented graphic designer. Married with young children of his own, he volunteered his time speaking to youth groups about the dangers of drug use and steering kids at risk toward a more productive life. I still remember how moving it was to be in this man's presence when he spoke of his mother, his wife, and his children. "I just want them to be proud of me." He took responsibility for his own choices, paid his debt to society, and then paid it forward through selfless acts of service. That is karma yoga.

The simplest definition I've read comes from Swami Vivekananda, who states that karma yoga is unselfishness, meaning not being attached to the fruits of your labor. Work is done purely out of service, without seeking outward fame and recognition, or even inner praise and conceit. A karma yogi acts not from a position of, "What's in it for me," but "How can I help?" I asked Roger Gabriel if someone is in service to others, yet amassing great material wealth, can he/she still be considered a Karmic yogi? "Yes," he said, "if that person is using that wealth for good."

Someone I'd describe as a karma yogi was Edythe Kirchmaier, known for her lifetime of giving back. She was a devoted volunteer at the disaster relief organization Direct Aid for more than 40 years until her recent death at the age of 107. I became familiar with this remarkable woman when I watched a short documentary snippet about her. At the age of 105, she became the oldest person, at the time, to join social media. She told of an incident when she was a child, where she had come home from school one day to ask her mother for some food to feed the poor children. Her mom was taken aback by her daughter's request, as her family was desperately poor, with barely enough food to feed her own family. But noticing the loving desire to help, her mom gave Edythe what little she had to take to the children. Edythe said, "People's attitudes have changed. We are more concerned about what we can get out of life, rather than what we can give. I think we can win over all of our adversities with love."

As Buddha said, "Better than a speech of a thousand vain words is one thoughtful word which brings peace to the mind." Even the words we utter are actions and have consequences. Neurologist, Ayurveda specialist, and cofounder of the Chopra Center Dr. David Simon used to tell his audiences, "When you speak, ask yourself, 'Is it true? Is it kind? Is it necessary?'"

What is your karmic legacy? All of your previous choices will lead you to your answer. Gandhi said, "I have learnt through bitter experience the one superior lesson to conserve my anger." Gandhi didn't say he suppressed or denied his anger. He conserved it, which is very different. He took action to support his intention for nonviolence, rather than fueling the rage and divisive behaviors.

In *Paradise Lost*, John Milton wrote, "The mind in its own place and in itself can make a heaven of hell or hell of heaven." When we learn to hold our inner dialogue accountable, that's when we are living in yoga. This is not the same thing as listening to our inner voice. Intelligence agencies call insignificant content on the Internet "chatter," and they weed through it to find relevant information. In the same way, the practice of yoga helps to fine tune the level of discernment to decipher between incessant chatter, which is a reflection of our ego (small self), and the messages we receive from our true inner voice (our higher self).

Living Yoga

Spend some time in silence. Observe your thoughts without judgment or attachment. Some of the things we say to ourselves, we wouldn't dream of saying out loud or to our best friends. So why not be your own best friend today? Witness your thoughts, and challenge yourself. How will you know the difference between your ego and your true self? Find a quiet, comfortable place where you won't be easily disturbed. Close your eyes. Draw your attention to your heart, and take a deep breath. When your intention is coming from a place of love, the search for the truth always results in a deep knowing.

Selfless service extends beyond just physical wants and needs. Vivekananda states, "Spirituality is the true basis of all our activities in life." Spiritual and intellectual knowledge passed on to others is also karma yoga. Dorothy Day, an American journalist, social activist, and Catholic convert, was an exemplary demonstration of someone who used her commitment to her faith to turn her own suffering into service. A native New Yorker, Day was born in 1897 and was witness to a tumultuous history. At a cost to her own personal freedom, Day was arrested multiple times after protesting for the rights of the underprivileged or speaking out against government-imposed injustices. Through her work as a devoted Catholic, she committed her life to kindness, gratitude, humbleness, honor, and service to the poor.

Vivekananda in describing karma yoga states, "It is the most difficult thing in this world to work and not care for the result, to help a man and never think that he ought to be grateful, to do some good work and at the same time never look to see whether it brings you name or fame, or nothing at all. Even the most arrant coward becomes brave when the world praises him."

Vivekananda said, "So when we ourselves work for the things of the world as slaves, there can be no love in us and our work is not 'true' work." Even work done out of obligation brings with it the opposite of love and fulfillment. Instead, there is hostility, restlessness, boredom, procrastination, carelessness. With self-awareness, we can make changes to our circumstances. By complaining about them, however, we only intensify the exact results we don't want.

> This is what Karma Yoga means: to be of help to everyone, without thought of return, and without asking questions. Never make a vain display of your gifts to the poor, or expect gratitude in return for your service to others, but rather always be grateful to them for giving you the occasion of practicing charity toward them. The true life of spiritual work is such a life of selfless service.
> (Swami Vivekananda)

When we shift the focus away from ourselves, our drama, and our problems and focus on others through acts of service, or extend kindness just for the sake of being kind, our lives are enriched with more hope, joy, and fulfillment. This may be tough for some caught up in the feverish era of the selfie and moment-by-moment self-serving posts for more "likes." However, practicing karma yoga doesn't mean that your act of service has to be some grand gesture. It can be something as kind as giving up your seat on the train for someone more in need without looking for praise or acknowledgment from others or even from yourself. Pick up a piece of trash off the ground, not because someone is watching but because it beautifies your landscape. It could also be as simple as not retweeting a mean post. To quote the prolific poet Maya Angelou, "When you know better, you do better."

Living Yoga

This exercise is actually a quote taken from the ancient text the *Dhammapada*, a collection of teachings from Buddha. "Do not give your attention to what others do or fail to do; give it to what you do or fail to do."

It's not an easy task to ask someone to spend the day in nonjudgment, let alone an entire lifetime. But if there is one moment today where you catch yourself judging and you can transform that analysis (good or bad) to acceptance or compassion and just shift your attention to your heart, you will understand self-awareness. Then act from this loving center. In the highly revered ancient poem the *Bhagavad Gita*, when Arjuna asks Krishna how to act, Krishna responds, "*Yogastha Kuru Karmani*. Perform work in this world, Arjuna, as a man established within himself, without selfish attachments, and alike in success and defeat. For yoga is perfect evenness of the mind."

Although I've experienced many trials and tribulations in this life, as I'm sure you have as well, most of the time, I feel really blessed. I see suffering so much greater than mine. I looked to my teacher Roger Gabriel for wisdom when going deeper into the idea of karma. I understand that my soul has chosen to embark upon these particular experiences in my life. But it seems an immeasurable task for someone who is a victim, or someone they love is the victim, of a heinous crime, to extend forgiveness to their perpetrator. How do you tell someone who was abused by her own father or the mother of that child who now suffers the anger, guilt, and shame of it that it's his or her karmic lot? There are those who transmute that pain through service and forgiveness, and then, there are others who never reach that state of consciousness. Roger responded, "You often cannot forgive the act, but you can always forgive the person who committed it."

That is truly living yoga when a mother of a murdered son stands in front of the killer and says, "I forgive you." Years ago, my friend Diana's mother was murdered during a home invasion in South Africa. Her mother's life was taken for a few material possessions, such as an old television set and a few pieces of silver. My friend spent several months before the trial saying, "The God in me forgives Mum's killers, and all is well."

As a Reiki master, Diana is trained in energetic healing and fully embraces the truth that we are all connected. Asking for divine help from angels, guides, and all the beings of light, she worked hard to release judgment, accept what was done, and find peace in her heart. During this time, her family had what most would consider the normal reactions of rage and vengeance for the criminals who took their mother's life. They were also very angry with Diana for her desire to come from a place of love and find forgiveness, which seemed preposterous to them at the time. As Diana tells it, "Connecting with God in the killers helped me to do the work. I also kept saying that God in me blesses God in you.

"When the day of the trial dawned, I was required to be in court to give evidence, and that is when the real work began. I was able to look at the killers, going cold at the fact that they were the ones I had seen in my psychic eye." Diana was the person to find her mother that dreadful day. As she placed her hands on her mother's already cold body, she had a vision of the men who did this. She identified them for the police, ultimately leading to their capture. "From my heart, I spoke to them, saying that the God in me forgives you."

She continued to share her experience with me. "During a recess, several black men came up to me to give condolences and said that they hoped the killers would hang. I replied that it was not for us to decide but for the court and that the cycle of hate had to stop now." This tragedy occurred during a tumultuous time with race relations in South Africa's history, given the recent and still unhealed wounds of Apartheid. Diana told these men, "If I want to live my life in fear and hate, then I would hate all black men, including you. So we must learn to accept that we are all one." Diana said that the men cried and thanked her. She told me, "This was a very special moment for me. I truly believe that this was a huge lesson for these men too."

Where does someone muster up this kind of strength? Years prior to her mom's murder, Diana had a near-death experience (NDE), where she remembers being given a choice whether to stay in the state of euphoria and pure divine love she was experiencing while her body remained in coma or return to her physical body and do what she was meant to do. She received very clear direction to use her gifts to become a healer. At the time, Diana was an elementary school teacher and had no formal training in any metaphysical modalities. She recounted the experience of how she thought of her children and chose to come back into her physical body and continue her life. Did this NDE prepare her for what was a remarkable demonstration of karma and bhakti yoga?

As my friend says, "There will always be sadness, but the shock and horror have subsided over the years." Because of her intention and desire to come from a place of love and her action to forgive, I believe Diana was granted divine grace that she carries with her in life today, in lieu of anger, bitterness and thoughts of revenge. This is the gift of yoga.

This next story, to me, truly exemplifies how to *live yoga*. My dear friend, who is a member of a popular Christian church in South Africa, shared with me an interaction between a priest and a distraught parishioner. The woman was lamenting how her eldest son was a thief. I remember being struck by the wisdom of the priest's response. Rather than empathize with her, or direct her to specific prayers to relieve her suffering, he held her accountable as he said, "How can you expect anything different from your son than for him to be a thief, when you fed him with stolen food?" It was common to hear how housekeepers would regularly "pinch" (steal) a spoonful of sugar, a spoonful of salt, or a handful of flour from their bosses, collecting the ingredients that would eventually add up to enough ingredients for a loaf of bread or a few scones. Call it karma, call it universal law, but all of your words, actions, and thoughts today create your tomorrow. What the priest was illustrating to his congregation was that, while this woman thought she was getting away with taking what did not belong to her, the fruit of her actions was ultimately great suffering as her son became a thief.

Stephen Hawking from the *Genius* series on PBS said, "Although we are each of us a product of the universe, the universe we live in is personal to us ... The universe is governed by the laws of nature. So we are responsible fully for the universe we live in." That's a tough pill to swallow if you are used to living in a mind-set where the world is out to get you, if you only ever shift the blame, and don't hold yourself accountable for your own actions.

Raja Yoga: the Royal Path (Meditation)

Referred to as the royal path, raja yoga offers a foundation of practices to direct our focus inward, rather than outward. As described in *The Seven Spiritual Laws of Yoga*, "The essence of Raja Yoga is an integration of mind, body and soul through procedures that enhance mind-body coordination ... Yoga is much more than a system of fitness. It is a science of balanced living." The great sage Patanjali described the goal of yoga as a path to total freedom from suffering. Buddha, Jesus, and many other sages, prophets, and spiritual leaders speak similarly that the way out of suffering is to get control of our fragile minds.

Although there is no definitive agreement on the biography of the ancient seer Maharishi Patanjali, he is credited with being the founder of the science and philosophy of yoga. The principles of yoga are defined in the work entitled *The Yoga Sutras of Patanjali*. In this classic work, Patanjali outlines eight components or eight limbs of yoga that provide a foundation for moving from beyond the ego, which binds us to suffering, to spirit, which is the real path to freedom and joy.

"The mind uncontrolled and unguided will drag us down forever —it will tear us apart, kill us; and the mind controlled and guided will save us, free us." Swami Vivekananda is not describing the techniques used by certain governments, religious fanatics, and other groups for the purpose of eliminating independent thinking, brainwashing, and using persuasion to gain power. Vivekananda is referring to raja yoga, the yoga of meditation, where union with the divine is achieved through practices that direct our awareness inward.

Raja yoga is the yoga of meditation. The practice of *dhyana*, meditation, helps us gain mastery over our minds, allowing us to gain mastery over the other seven limbs. We then operate from self-referral rather than object referral. From this place, the other paths of yoga merge into and work in unison with the others. This is why raja yoga is referred to as the royal path, because it is the framework for all other yoga paths.

I, like many, imagined that meditation was reserved for only the most virtuous and they held the secret to what it really was. They had something special that the rest of us weren't able to tap into— or so we thought. I had always been curious about meditation, finding myself in workshops, researching on the Internet, and learning simple techniques with my Pilates instructor, but I still questioned whether I was doing it correctly. I did recognize that the meditative style of Pilates and yoga I was practicing was resonating with me like no other physical fitness activity ever had. Years later, I happened upon the free online meditation challenge guided by Dr. Deepak Chopra, and I committed to *The 21-Day Meditation Challenge*, participating twice a day. A few months later, I registered for my first Chopra Center event, which was an intensive weeklong meditation retreat, which would prove to be the inception of my journey back to my self, to my truth, to my authentic life.

Along with the various sessions with keynote speakers, group meditations, yoga classes, and other activities scheduled, there was an optional sunrise meditation set up outdoors on the terrace lawn. The resort where the event was being held was sold out, so I was booked at one of the nearby resorts, which required that I be ready and out of my hotel room by 5:00 a.m. to catch the shuttle if I was going to make it to meditation in time. Blanket in tow, I'd make the brisk, chilly walk to the lawn, aware of the moments right before dawn that felt like a "pregnancy" of what might emerge that day. It's where I first met Wendi, who I'd later find out was called Mama Bear, which was perfect because when she led sunrise meditation, you could feel Wendi's love rippling throughout, and she truly left you feeling nourished. We'd complete our meditation and open our eyes to a greeting of a thin, dewy mist fizzing up from the resort's putting green in front of us as the sun would now be rising beyond the mountains. We'd all receive a burst of pure energy that no caffeinated drink could provide. A few days in, I approached Wendi at the end of our morning meditation to express my gratitude for her presence and her guidance. She shared with me that this particular event, called Seduction of Spirit, was also her first experience with a sunrise meditation. And then she said, "I've participated in fifteen of these events, and I haven't missed a sunrise meditation since." I remember thinking, *Wow, I get it*. Wendi remains one of my first and truest inspirations for following through on my own commitment to a regular practice of meditation.

Through the years, Wendi has been very generous with sharing her journey with her own health challenges, including chronic pain, and her remarkable path of healing as a result of meditation and her commitment to living a life in yoga. It left an indelible impression on me because I had also been dealing with chronic nerve pain for more than fifteen years. By the end of that weeklong retreat, I had gained clarity and hope that I, too, had found a path to healing.

When I began my training at the Chopra Center, I was curious why raja yoga was considered the royal path. Again, this cannot be an intellectual exercise. I can teach, advise, even discipline someone on a path toward a healthier lifestyle, but if that person doesn't take the first step, all the theory in the world will not intellectualize him or her into the skinny jeans gathering dust in the closet or get him or her to take responsibility for his or her own health and wellbeing. Manipulating, guilting, shaming, or even giving an ultimatum to someone in hopes of them giving up cigarettes or other nicotine products has never worked. I watched my mom nag my dad pretty much my entire life while he was alive. Yes, the intention behind my mother's incessant lecturing, pleading, crying, and yelling on the surface may have been out of love, but the truth is it had nothing to do with love. It was all about fear, fear that he would get sick and die. Sadly, that was exactly the outcome of more than fifty years of my father's nicotine addiction. It's easy for those of us on the sidelines to state the obvious about someone else's habits, vices, and behaviors, but we cannot will the change or force feed the knowledge or resolution. Ultimately, the person has to do his/her own work. Chinese philosopher and sage Lao Tzu observed, "The ordinary man must make a spiritual start somewhere, sometime ... The journey of a thousand miles begins with the first step."

In the same way, during my certification programs in meditation, yoga, and Ayurvedic lifestyle, I began, with feverish excitement, to absorb as much of the knowledge as I could from the study manuals and recommended reading. My nightstand was slowly disappearing under the tower of books and Vedic texts. But the real shift for me came when my meditation and yoga asana practice became as regular as my morning tea; and when I began, step by step, implementing new health tools into my daily life. It's when I recognized the perfection of yoga and began using yoga as my compass. When I say the perfection of yoga, I mean the science of yoga, a philosophy of life that has held up for thousands of years. I am still human, and I am reorienting the compass all day, every day to keep on course. It is not a quick fix but a commitment to practicing that allows a path of freedom to unfold. This path is clearly outlined in the eight limbs of yoga. That's why it's called a practice, because as humans we constantly fall, get back up, only to fall again. But with yoga as my compass, I believe both the fall and rise can be done with divinely granted grace.

One of the key practices of following raja, the royal path of yoga, is meditation, which leads to spontaneous right action, and then all the paths of yoga become integrated in one's life. Your ability to maintain equanimity grows, even in the face of crisis or chaos. You effortlessly become more self-aware; you begin to detach from defending your viewpoint; and you experience less judgment of yourself and others, continually being brought back to the present moment. It becomes easier to find gratitude, joy, love, and peace in everything. Like the Vietnamese Buddhist monk Thich Nhat Hanh says, even the act of washing dishes can be your meditation if you allow yourself to stay in the moment. What exactly does it mean to stay in the moment? Author and spiritual teacher Eckhart Tolle says it is a misconception of our human minds to believe that life should not be challenging. We spend a great deal of time complaining about the "could haves," "should haves," and "would haves," rather than accepting the "isness of things," as Tolle calls it.

The effects and benefits of a regular meditation practice can be seen outside of the meditation itself. As we begin to see our desires fulfilled more easily, we become more aware and our intuition is heightened. We begin to cultivate more feelings of appreciation, happiness, joy, and calm. We become less reactive. Some changes can be seen immediately, such as better and higher quality of sleep, reduced anxiety, and lowered blood pressure. Other changes are more subtle and take longer to be assimilated into one's life. An overall sense of wellbeing is also evidence that meditation is having positive effects. Personally, I have seen dramatic personal transformation as a result of living a yogic lifestyle, which includes my regular meditation practice.

As a result of meditation, I was very fortunate to see a dramatic acceleration in recovery following major back surgery. I meditated before I entered the operating room and multiple times a day for weeks following. With the permission of my surgeon, I was able to get back on the yoga mat within six weeks. I made sure not to compromise the surgery, but I was thrilled to participate in daily yoga classes while I completed my certification to become a Chopra Center certified instructor. I put into practice all of the teachings I would share with my students, including nonjudgment, patience, and trust in the process as I healed.

I find myself calmer, less mercurial, more vibrant, and more content. Uncomfortable, volatile, or awkward situations are now few and far between, and meditation allows me to diffuse the ones that do present themselves in my life. I am human, and my ego can still get the best of me, but the rebound time back to a centered place within me is remarkably shorter. I am kinder to myself, and I no longer play the relentless reel of negative thoughts, judging, and criticizing or doubting myself. Meditation has given me permission to have own my truth and stand in my light.

Because it was becoming my own experience, I was able to understand why raja yoga is called the royal path: karma, bhakti and jnana all become merged into my philosophy. Am I being yogic in all my thoughts, words, and actions? The most challenging for me comes in conversations where judgment, criticism, sarcasm, and passive aggressive behaviors seem so prevalent. Without any self-awareness, the melodramas played out in daily life are accepted as normal, and some people can navigate with little or no awareness, no accountability, or any attempt at true listening. So then, it becomes my challenge to keep my equanimity and stay in a place of love, remembering that my intention is to come from the heart. In his book, *The Path to Love*, Dr. Chopra writes, "There is no single road to this quietness of meditation, yet to be genuine, any meditation must take the mind beyond its superficial nature, which is restless and chaotic, to its deeper nature as the peace that passes all understanding."

> Purity of heart, mind and body is absolutely the basic principle, the bedrock upon which the building of Godliness rests ... Therefore, we must remember that external practices have value only as they help to develop personal purity ... The person whose heart never holds even the thought of harm to anyone is a true yogi. (Swami Vivekananda)

The goal of yoga is to deepen our connection to our souls by integrating all the layers of our being—body, mind, spirit, and environment. These eight limbs are entry points to expanded awareness through knowing ourselves as more than just the body/mind where only the desires and needs of our five senses are fulfilled. Operating from this space, we may believe we will achieve happiness, but because these external acquisitions are impermanent, happiness then becomes momentary and fleeting. By becoming aware of ourselves as unbounded, unchanging spirit, our lives then become directed by conscious choice making and an expanded sense of self through our interpretations, choices, and experiences that come from the deeper level of our true nature and our divinity.

Eight Limbs of Yoga

> But there are subtler laws that rule the hidden spiritual planes and the inner realm of consciousness; these principles are knowable through the science of yoga.
> —Swami Vivekananda

The eight limbs of yoga provide a practical guide toward wholeness, with integration of the physical, emotional, spiritual, psychological, and environmental layers of life leading to divine union—yoga. Here is a brief overview of these eight limbs.

Yamas

Most, if not all, religious traditions embolden living with the highest moral code, and the edicts are often presented in ways that bound them, and the person attempting to observe them, to external duty. You should do this, or you shouldn't do that, with guilt, shame, retribution, and punishment looming. In describing the first limb, called the yamas, the great sage Patanjali says that as you become more self-aware and direct your focus inward, there is an evolution toward spontaneous "right" behavior. When your ego is no longer controlling your actions, you ultimately lose the capacity to harm yourself or others.

You naturally observe the moral virtues that form the blueprint for yoga practice: *ahimsa* (nonviolence), *satya* (truthfulness), *asteya* (non-stealing), *brahmacharya* (sexual restraint), and *aparigraha* (generosity). When you are at peace within yourself, practicing ahimsa or nonviolence with all of creation comes naturally. This is considered to be the highest of the moral codes because when a person is truly established in peace, there can only be love and compassion. Gandhi, Martin Luther King Jr., Nelson

Mandela, and Thich Naht Hanh all aimed to have their message heard through nonviolence. Patanjali describes *satya* or truth as integrity in all thoughts, words, and actions. However, if being truthful means harming someone else, ancient wisdom declares it is better to remain quiet and say nothing. This ancient wisdom is still relevant today, particularly with the rampant social media culture of cyberbullying. I heard throughout my life, "If you have nothing nice to say, don't say anything at all." *Brahmacharya* is often simply described as celibacy. However, in a more expanded view, it represents channeling sexual and creative forces in ways that honor our highest self. Coming from a place of pure love, one becomes more discerning in the expression of sexual and/or creative energies. There are people who choose to devote their lives to abstinence, but observing this yama includes respect for ourselves and others by exhibiting responsible behavior. *Aparigraha* is more than just the act of being generous. Trust in the abundance of the universe to provide dissolves any need to hoard, be greedy, or exploit others or situations for your own favor. Fear of losing, not having enough, or feeling jealous of someone else's good fortune are all traps of the ego as we compare ourselves to others. Generosity can be extended in various ways beyond gifts, such as a kind gesture, in being fully present with someone, or in donating your time or talent to help or serve.

Niyamas

The second limb of yoga refers to our personal behavior, taking accountability for it, and holding ourselves responsible for our own deeds. This doesn't mean we operate from a critical pedestal but more from a commitment to attending to our own code of living from the level of our souls. My favorite description of the niyamas is one that asks the following two questions. How do you live when no one is watching? What choices do you make when you are the only witness? When living a heart-centered life, one that is natural and balanced, our ego personality transforms, and the qualities of *saucha* (purity), *santosha* (contentment), *tapas* (discipline), *svadhyaya* (self-study), and *isvara-pranidhana* (celebration of and devotion to God) emerge. We no longer seek or need self-destructive behaviors that only bring us suffering. It's no secret that when we live a healthy, balanced life, in harmony with universal or natural law, we effortlessly choose nourishment over toxicity. This includes practicing discipline with overindulgences of all the senses. With the mind, we experience these excesses in the form of being overly critical, self-sabotaging, and remaining in victim consciousness ("poor me" syndrome) with ourselves, along with participating in toxic acts like gossip, judgment of others, and malicious intent. These Niyamas or personal practices lead to an inner journey of self-discovery where our value is no longer coming from external forces.

The first two limbs of yoga help us navigate how we show up for our life and how we conduct ourselves as part of society with a framework of morality. So, how do we cultivate the evolution of spontaneous "right" living? Patanjali outlines practical steps on the path of yoga as purification, refinement, and surrender. These steps help to abolish the causes of suffering: ignorance of our real nature; egoism; attachment, which he defines as "clinging to pleasure"; aversion, "clinging to pain"; and fear of death, "which makes us cling to life."

The remaining six limbs of yoga, when practiced consciously, help to purify our minds, bodies, and spirits; refine our senses by raising our awareness of our true nature; and finally, with nourishment, clarity, and balance, we can surrender into trusting our pure potential and creating joyful lives, even beyond the wildest dreams of our ego selves. Again, the eight limbs are not sequential to be followed like a checklist. For me, they are a compass to steer me away from the limitations of my ego and conditioned mind toward a more expanded reality and understanding of the true nature of life. Yoga allows me to experience life's real magic.

Asana

Patanjali describes *asana* as mastering the body. Translated as seat, *asanas* or yoga postures, were originally created and used to ready the body for meditation so ancient yogis could sit still and silent for extended periods. These *asanas* were also a tool to understand the connection between mind, body, and spirit. Just as nature surrenders to the ebb and flow of life, yoga poses offer this same intelligence through contracting and releasing; flexing and stretching; balancing and enduring. Our bodies gain flexibility, strength, and endurance with the physical activity of yoga. If we take the same approach we use on the yoga mat and incorporate those principles into our daily lives off the mat, we will see the same qualities come forth, including flexibility of the mind, strength of character, and endurance, balance, and calm even in the midst the chaos.

Acceptance doesn't mean passivity. It means making a decision not to fight the flow. Being aware of our actions, words, and thoughts allows the space to let it flow, making decisions that spontaneously create a more fluid life. On the mat, when we struggle or strain while making our way into a particular yoga pose, we will, more often than not, experience pain and injury. Even the intention to allow your body to take whatever expression of that pose means acceptance, non-judgment, and surrender. In the same way, when we detach from how we think life is supposed to be, or release trying to control outcomes, and accept how things are in that moment, we step into the natural flow of life.

Pranayama

> For breath is life, and if you breathe well you will live long on earth.
> —Sanskrit proverb

One way to understand the natural flow of life is to observe our breath. The simplest example of the essence of *prana* is our breath. Ancient yogis knew the power of *prana* or life force and developed conscious exercises or practices to control and direct the breath. These techniques are known as *pranayama* and include ones to energize, relax, cool, and generate heat, among others.

We are offered continuous opportunities to live in the moment. By becoming aware of our breath, we realize that each inhale brings the potential for something new, while each exhale allows us to expel the old and the stale, the stuff that no longer serves us. When our minds are calm, our breath will follow. And when our minds are turbulent, our breathing will follow suit. As you can imagine, if our breath is continually turbulent, stunted, or shallow, our bodies are deprived of vital oxygen and nourishment (*prana*), which eventually leads to illness. Practicing *pranayama* is a powerful way to create balance in both hemispheres of our brains; provide sustenance by cleansing, balancing, and invigorating our physical bodies; calm the nervous system; as well as help to quiet our mental unrest.

The breath is our source of power in the practice of yoga as we synchronize the breath to the action or movement. When we are holding our breath or straining through a particular pose on the mat, we are depriving our bodies from vital oxygen needed to nourish our cells. *Pranayama* exercises help to strengthen our lung capacity as we focus on the intake of oxygen with each inhale and the release of carbon monoxide and other toxins with each exhale. Learning breath control has many benefits. For example, in a stressful situation when the pulse increases and the rhythm of the breath speeds up and becomes shallow, we can reverse the negative effects on our physiology by practicing a few rounds of relaxing *pranayama* techniques. An advanced technique in *pranayama* is the practice of *bandhas* (Sanskrit for lock or stop) where holding the breath stops blood flow temporarily to a particular area of the body. When the *bandha* is released, a new blood supply is directed to that area, nourishing, replenishing, purifying, and releasing any energetic blockages.

Pratyahara

Go inward to master control of the senses. As Drs. Deepak Chopra and David Simon explain in *The Seven Spiritual Laws of Yoga*, "*Pratyahara* is the process of temporarily withdrawing the senses from the outer world in order to recognize the sensations of your inner world." This practice of retreating from the outer sensory world allows us to gain clarity, enhance our intuitive abilities, which we all possess, and appreciate the little things in life more easily and with more joy. In today's fast-paced, ever-changing, rapid-fire sensory overload, we lose our connection to the natural rhythms of life. The initial removal of social media feeds can send some people into a real panic, where the body responds as if it really is a life-or-death situation, the fight-or-flight response. Given a bit of time to allow those fears to dissipate, a wave of peace arises, and space is created. Withdrawal of our senses is not meant to imply deprivation. When we refine our senses in the practice of *pratyahara*, our senses are heightened, and we become more in tune with the more subtle senses, deepening the connection between mind, body, and soul. In this way, we lose our cravings for toxic behaviors, and we easily gravitate to more nourishing choices.

Dharana

Have you ever been so focused on a particular task or completely engrossed in a moment, oblivious to everything else going on around you? Concentration is the essence of *dharana*. "Where our attention goes, energy flows." "What we resist persists." When we practice focusing our attention, we are training our minds to relinquish control and attachment to the thousands of thoughts that race through our minds. By steadying the mind on a single point of focus, we learn to master intention and attention in our lives, and we are more easily able to manifest our deepest desires.

Dhyana

Amid change, your soul is always a constant. This never-ending presence is who you really are. Through the practice of meditation, you gain access to this truth and find the essence of your true self. Meditation develops the ability to become the observer of your thoughts, feelings, emotions, sensation, and sounds, without the need to react. *"Dhyana* is the cultivation of your awareness so that in the midst of this unending change, you do not lose yourself in the objects of your experience." A regular practice of meditation nurtures stillness and silence, creating the space for new possibilities, creative solutions, and a settled mind to emerge. Meditation allows us to take the qualities of the spirit, like calm, clarity, peace, love, and gratitude, with us into our daily lives. Buddha expresses this in his teachings: "They are wise whose thoughts are steady and minds serene, unaffected by good and bad. They are awake and free from fear."

Samadhi

When we transcend ego and merge completely with the divine, we've reached enlightenment. Enlightenment is not a place. *"Samadhi* is a state of being settled in pure, unbounded awareness." For the thinking mind, it is incomprehensible to perceive a world beyond this local domain. However, there have been teachers in our recent past, such as Buddha and Jesus Christ, who reached unity consciousness, seeing beyond and through the veil of ego to the truth that we are all one; we are all connected. "If you think you are enlightened, spend some time with your family." This quote illustrates how we are always traversing the layers of life, going from higher states of consciousness to our ego and intellect and back again.

In an article entitled, *The Eight Limbs, the Core of Yoga,* writer William J.D. Doran wrote, "Yoga does not seek to change the individual; rather, it allows the natural state of total health and integration in each of us to become a reality." There are many ways where people are being yogic without actually knowing. However, their lives are demonstrations of the essence of yoga. Maybe we say that we are being good Christians, Jews, Muslims, or other religious devotees. Or we know we are loyal members of our families and communities. Or we know we are a devoted friend. What does being in yoga look like in our daily lives?

- Being faithful even in the face of temptation
- Devoting one's life to family without complaint—true joy from that role, joy even in the mundane
- Living in authenticity—following your passion
- Extending kindness to strangers—even in the face of scorn
- Obeying personal and societal laws when no one is watching
- Committing to nonjudgment—avoidance of gossip or nowadays avoiding reactivity or deliberate cyberbullying, "clapping back," or "throwing shade"
- Respecting one's health
- Volunteering without the need for approval from others
- Accepting someone's grace, generosity, and help
- Living with integrity with your words, thoughts, and actions
- Diffusing, rather than escalating, fear and hatred
- Choosing forgiveness

THREE

Nature's Intelligence

Whether we do it consciously or unconsciously, we are all trying to unfold our divinity. Oftentimes, when coming from a pure heart, people's actions, words, and thoughts demonstrate the core principle of being in union without even knowing they are practicing yoga. They are in yoga. Nature is one of the easiest ways to realize yoga as we stand in reverence of the beauty of God, spirit, source, universe, or the higher self. That union takes your breath away, or better saying, it engulfs your whole being with the breath and breadth of life, called *prana* in Sanskrit.

When we awake to our own true nature, we realize the connectedness, the oneness we have with the entire universe. When Mark Nepo says this nature is "dormantly potent," you can feel the possibilities, the pure potential, and the creative power resting within all of us. What follows is a life that flows effortlessly, not without its challenges and lessons. However, in yoga, we can relinquish the struggle, the suffering, and the resistance against life's natural flow, harmony, and grace.

"The perfected Bhakta no longer goes to see God in temples and churches; he knows no place where he will not find (God)."

My mom visited a couple times while I lived in South Africa, but on this particular trip, I was very excited to show her some of the natural beauty that is part of why it's referred to as "the beloved country." We traveled to all the main spots on the Panorama Route in Mpumalanga, a bit of heaven on earth, where two rivers converge and have carved out some of the most beautiful sites, including canyons, spectacular waterfalls, and mountain formations. Lively outdoor markets color the landscape, with street vendors selling their arts and crafts while talking and singing in the local dialect. We sat at one spot overlooking a view that truly takes your breath away. As we sat there, I could tell my mom wasn't really present.

She said, "I just realized it is Sunday and I didn't go to church." I could feel myself wanting to be offended at how my efforts to give her an amazing experience were going unnoticed. Instead, I motioned for my mom to adjust her seated position ever so slightly and asked her to look up.

I said, "Mom, look around for a moment. If you cannot feel God's presence here, no brick-and-mortar building is going to do that for you."

We happened to be sitting atop a mesa looking out at the vista known as God's Window. My mom's eyes filled with tears, and in recognition of the gift before her, she humbly responded, "Thank you." Without needing to utter another word, we sat in awe together. We were connected to ourselves, each other, and everything around us, and it was the same heartbeat in sync. That is yoga. I remember this story in gratitude, and I marvel at how nature can be one our greatest teachers about present moment awareness.

We see the divine intelligence of nature all around us and within us, the union and wholeness of the universe. However, too often it is drowned out by distractions, or it is overlooked, ignored, dismissed, or rebelled against, only to discover in hindsight the power of the infinite wisdom. William Shakespeare wrote, "One touch of nature makes the whole world kin." When we are paying attention and we remember that we, too, are nature, we feel the connection and unity, the yoga, with everything. Even if only briefly, time and space become warped or no longer exist.

My mom and I were booked at one of the self-catering bungalows at Lower Sabie Rest Camp in Kruger National Park. By that time, I had become very fond of bird watching and carried my book, my list of species sighted, and a couple sets of binoculars. When first arriving in South Africa, I wondered why bird watching was such a big deal in the country. You only need to be driving along the N3 highway and spot a flock of long-tailed paradise whydahs to understand. I grew up in New Jersey, where the occasional spotting of a cardinal or blue jay would be a thrill. But with more than nine hundred species in Southern Africa, I quickly began my love affair with the spectacular bird life. I was often teased for asking the game rangers to stop the truck until everyone else on the drive got sight of the carmine bee eater or the lilac-breasted roller. The vibrancy of the colors nature offers is indescribable but is always show stopping for me.

The camp was nothing fancy, but it was well equipped for moments of solace, where nature's rhythm eventually coaxed calm into even the most neurotic of minds. Hard to conceive now, but this was pre-data cell phones or social media. I convinced my mom to enjoy her lunch outside on the picnic table outside of our bungalow. Of course, my bird book and binoculars were in tow. Beyond the fence, we were delighted to see some herbivore passers-by, including waterbuck, kudu, and buffalo. But above us, we also got quite the visual treat while crested barbets flew from tree to tree. As we allowed nature to recalibrate our vibrations, I began to hear a tiny, continuous knocking and knew I had to spot the woodpecker responsible for that sound. To my surprise, there were two! I was privy to a rare event and had spotted both the male and female, and I was thrilled. Time elapsed without us even noticing. That's the power of nature to heal our spirit.

The following morning, we were up by 4:30 a.m. for an early

game drive and set out at 5:00 a.m. to the meeting place. In the dark, barely able to see, we sensed we were being followed but couldn't quite figure out what it was until the unmistakable sound of laughter could be heard. Although I felt a shiver of fear run down my spine, I convinced my mom that we were behind electric fences and we needn't worry. There would be safety in numbers once we reached the meeting point and other guests also started to arrive. As we waited for the rangers to show up, we all turned toward the camp's ablutions area, where a young woman was running from the restroom screaming. Apparently our stalking hyena had made its way to the bathrooms, giving this woman quite the morning fright. The ranger told us that the same hyena had been relocated fifty kilometers farther north but made its way back to what it knew to be its home territory. Everyone forgot about needing coffee since adrenaline was now pumping enough energy throughout our bodies as we set out eagerly to see what nature would unveil to us at dawn.

Among the many blessed sightings on that crisp morning, the ranger and his tracker spotted a very mature male elephant up ahead. This bull, as the males are called, would be one of the largest I'd see during my years living in South Africa, probably weighing close to seven tons! The ranger crept slowly closer as we all leaned with our cameras to photograph this great giant. The elephant changed direction and walked slowly and silently alongside the road toward our vehicle. What happened next would be indelibly stamped in my memory. In a split second, the bull turned, spread his ears, and faced our truck. I don't think I had any thoughts at that moment as I clicked my camera, lowered my hands, and stood in absolute stillness and silence as we were locked eye to eye. My mom would tell me later that everyone else, including she, had bolted to the other side of the truck, more out of instinct than the illusion that they would be any safer. I can still feel this bull's presence in my mind's eye. Later, other guests would ask if I was afraid, but I don't remember feeling any fear. I felt only love. Words cannot fully capture what I experienced as this majestic animal and I shared breath and we were connected. I was humbled and filled with an overwhelming amount of gratitude as he shook his head and walked away. I had that photo enlarged and framed to remind me of my own inner strength and power and that fear is often only a creation of our minds.

You don't need to travel somewhere else, or do anything at all, to have these moments of connection, union, or yoga. We can find them in the now, in the present moment, in the glory of the ordinary. When we become aware of our divine nature, we start to notice the divine in even the smallest wonders of our lives, even the mundane.

Living Yoga

- Get "lost" or get "found" in a great piece of music. The combination of great lyrics and a tune that resonates with you has enormous power to transcend the ego. This is best done with music that touches our heart in a healing way, rather than one that allows our ego to ruminate over past regressions, those of our own or of someone else's.

- The next time you get to the beach, just sit with your eyes closed and listen to the melody of the waves of the ocean.

- Sit silently in nature and become aware of how you are nature—in sync with the rhythms. You begin to recognize that your heartbeat is the same heartbeat of the universe.

- Take a few moments to observe your environment. See the blessing in the ordinary. Wake up just before dawn; sit outside and witness the sunrise, even if you can't see it. Take in the sights and sounds as nature greets the morning.

- Or simply close your eyes and put your attention on your breath. As the contemporary spiritual leader Eckhart Tolle explains, the breath only lives in the present. You cannot reclaim your breath from the past, nor can you breathe for yourself in the future. Breathing happens right now. Be with your breath and you will understand what it means to be in the present moment, in union with nature's intelligence, in yoga.

I heard on one of Oprah Winfrey's shows that our animals can be our greatest teachers. Eckhart Tolle says in his book *Guardians of Being: Spiritual Teachings from our Dogs and Cats*, "If you want to understand true present moment awareness, one of the ways to do that is spend a few moments with your pet." I'm of the belief that anyone who says, "It's just a dog," or "It's just a cat" has never actually been truly present with one. This can be said of many animals, not just our domestic pets.

Spending time with my dog, Themba, can definitely provide a source of comic relief in my life. (Thembalethu is his full South African Khosa tribal name, meaning Hope—pronounced Tembaletu.) When I'm feeling vulnerable or sad, I'll look him in the eyes, feeling the connection on a soul level with him. And a split second later, he is turning his head to lean down and clean his private parts. That's living in the present moment at its best. Themba reminds me often to heed my teacher's words: "Don't take yourself so seriously."

I got Themba as a pup ten days before leaving South Africa after living there for nearly seven years. A couple of days before we left the country, we stayed at a pet-friendly hotel in Cape Town, and I remember laying on the couch sobbing as a moment of deep sadness washed over me with the reality that I would be leaving this country that had become embedded in my heart forever. As I lay there with my eyes closed, tears rolling down my cheeks, I was suddenly snapped out of my own emotion with Themba kissing me on my cheek. When I opened my eyes, my pup was looking at me in a way that I can only describe as a feeling of compassion. He walked back to his bed and fell back to sleep. I was in awe that my eight-week-old puppy could already be so present with me. He continues to be a great barometer of my internal well-being.

Some might say I have a vivid imagination. Maybe so. I don't dispute this, nor do I try to defend it. I know the truth of this story, and I share it as an example of how one can be guided by God, trust in the divine intelligence, if one is open, ready, curious, and willing to expand the level of consciousness. It was during the same time as I was struggling with a pivotal decision in my life, where my voice was either going to rise from within me and be heard or it would be stifled in the expectations, persuasions, and demands of someone else's dream.

My dog was suffering from recurring ear infections, always in his left ear. It could just be a coincidence, but in spiritual circles, the left side is representative of the feminine energy. It was frustrating and expensive constantly trying to figure out what was causing my dog's infections. It caused so much stress for us, as he was afraid and also hated having fluids squirted in his ears. And for me, there was so much distress trying to administer this kind of treatment.

It was a quiet moment, early in the day, when I sat with my pup, talking to him about this ear problem. I was desperate to figure it out as I couldn't bear seeing him like this, depressed and shaking his head violently to relieve the itching and pain. Our pets are always in the present moment. You only need to watch them for a few minutes and you will also find yourself in the now. We've all heard the stories of dogs diagnosing cancer in their owners before the doctors; alerting their owners of an oncoming seizure; or sensing and rescuing family members from dangerous and potentially fatal situations. Themba has done these types of things on several occasions: protecting my friend as he detected a sonic boom before it was audible to our human ears and catching a burglar in the neighborhood and sending a warning message to all the neighborhood dogs. After I came home from my back surgery, he never left my side that first day, even refusing to take care of his basic needs and fiercely guarding me.

In a deeply connected moment, completely present with Themba, as he looked at me, I noticed he tilted his head. Up until this point, I attributed that tilt to the pain and irritation of his ear infection. But in that timeless moment, I had a flash of insight, and I said out loud, "Themba, what is it you are trying to tell me with this ear infection? What am I not hearing?" What was revealed to me in the asking of that question changed the trajectory of my life forever. Less than twenty-four hours after that interaction, Themba's ear infection completely cleared up. I love the quote, "When the student is ready, the teacher will appear." Nature's intelligence is magical when one tunes into it. In that desperate moment of wanting answers, I was open to the gift of clarity and healing, for not only my dog's ears, but for my own path.

FOUR

Meditation and the Gift of Silence

"God is Harmony; the devotee who attunes himself will never perform any action amiss." Paramahansa Yogananda so beautifully defines the real purpose of meditation, where we feel connected, centered and in alignment with natural law. As he says, there is no better "inward protection." In meditation, we wake up our higher consciousness and the rest of the paths of yoga merge together as a natural way of life. Old behaviors no longer control our choices.

"In the still mind, in the depths of meditation, the self reveals itself."

Psalm 46:10 says, "Be still and know that I am God." The goal of the science of yoga is to obtain the necessary stillness by which one may truly know God. Psalm 23 repeats the same theme of peace, calm, and stillness: "God leads me to still waters that restore my spirit." These still waters are always there. God is always there. We just have to peel back the layers of conditioning and silence the outer and inner chatter so we can hear the truth. The *Bhagavad Gita* says, "These bodies are perishable; but the dweller in these bodies is eternal." Meister Eckhart said, "Nothing in all creation is so like God as silence."

I called upon Roger Gabriel, a Vedic scholar who is my teacher, my trusted advisor and friend, for many conversations while I was writing this book. Roger grew up Christian in Liverpool, England, as part of the Anglican Church but said his family was not particularly religious. They attended church on Sundays and major holidays, but it wasn't forced upon him. He recalled being about eight or nine years old when he came upon an article entitled *Roof of the World* in the school library. It was the period just before China's invasion of Tibet, so he was aware of what was going on in that part of the world. He remembers even as a small child having a fascination with India and Tibet, an affinity he's carried with him throughout his life.

The evolution toward Roger's spiritual awakening came in his mid-twenties, when he discovered meditation. Up until that point, less-than-healthy habits and being under high stress were normal parts of life. More than four decades have passed since that first introduction to meditation, and Roger has since taught thousands of students all over the world. He is a respected Vedic scholar and appeased his childhood curiosities with frequent travel to India and Tibet. He is involved with various charity programs in India, including having a pivotal role in rebuilding the school of the *ashram* (Sanskrit for hermitage or place of retreat) to which he belongs. Roger currently serves as a Chopra Center master educator and is a member of the Chopra Center Certification's Advisory Board. He teaches regularly at Chopra Center workshops, seminars, and teacher training programs.

With more than forty years of meditation experience, both in his own personal practice and his work as a teacher and scholar, Roger Gabriel has been a special teacher, inspiration, guide, and mentor to me. Personally, I felt a shift in my learning, in the understanding of integrating yoga into my life when I met Roger while training to become a teacher of Primordial Sound Meditation (PSM) at the Chopra Center. I remember there being a compassion and eloquence in the way he spoke about meditation, and I easily sensed the honor and responsibility of passing this knowledge on or helping others to remember it for themselves. "Remembering is not an intellectual exercise," he says. "It's an experience." In interviewing Roger for this book, most vivid for me is his genuineness, the passion and service, the love and devotion, and the lightheartedness with which he approaches life. He says, "What does enlightenment mean? It means to lighten up, so don't take yourself too seriously."

I remember at the certification program a particular student, who I'll call Bill. Bill was almost a caricature of himself. He was incredibly bright, very dedicated to learning, and extremely devoted to his own path toward health and fitness. In looking back now, I smile as I remember him. Aside from the fact that he was obviously smitten with one of my dear friends, who was also a student of PSM at the same time as I, you'd always see Bill rushing about, whizzing by the lobby of the resort, wearing only bike shorts and a sleeveless workout shirt, always looking like he was late for something.

Bill was always the first to approach Roger after class, in what seemed like an aggressive attempt to have all of his questions about life answered in those brief moments. Roger kept his cool, and as always, he gave this man his complete presence and attention, no matter how relentlessly the questions were fired at him. I think it was just Bill's passion and hunger for knowledge that made his approach seem so intense. He'd challenge Roger with questions about transcendence and an omnipotent God, about the local or physical domain and the nonlocal or infinite realm and the fundamentals of our true existence. I was also very eager to hear the responses as I waited to fulfill my own curiosity. Bill would get very exasperated by the matter-of-fact responses Roger would deliver.

"It's not an intellectual exercise. You cannot rationalize this with your mind. God cannot be encapsulated in our human thought. It's when we transcend thought where we experience God."

Bill would fire back, "Have you experienced this transcendence?"

Roger would calmly say, "Yes." It was almost comical to see the wheels of Bill's mind working as he remained frustrated. Roger would offer the same advice over and over: "Meditate on it."

"Now you must realize that truth directly and immediately. Then only will your heart be free from any doubt ... the only absolute proof is direct and immediate experience within your own soul." The great Indian sage Adi Shankara is explaining here that guidance from scriptures and from our teachers is of great value in providing a road map, but as Dr. Deepak Chopra asks, "If I point at the moon, are you going to worship my finger?" It is only in the "direct illumination" of our own truth, our own consciousness, our own soul where we accurately know God.

"The treasure that I have found there cannot be described in words. The mind cannot conceive of it." Trying to intellectualize others into understanding the kind of celebration of God I experience is ineffective. Accepting my truth as their own is not the goal anyway. A Persian proverb says, "Seek truth in meditation, not in moldy books. Look in the sky to find the moon, not in the pond."

The "beginner's mind" refers to approaching a new skill or sport with excitement and openness, without preconceived ideas, without anticipated outcomes. In Buddhism, it's called *Shoshin*. With nothing to compare it to, new meditators often have the ability to transcend thought without trying. That's how I remember it when I first practiced meditation. And then the mind interjects: *I should be getting in "the gap." I should be having deeper experiences. Why is my mind racing? Yesterday's meditation was so much better.* The judgment of my meditation came from waiting for some experience to happen, or expectations of how it was supposed to be. I then remind myself that if I want to see if meditation is working, I just need to take a look at my life outside of meditation.

My teachers always stressed that it's not what happens in the twenty- to thirty-minute meditation but what's happening in your life outside of meditation. Are you less reactive, more reflective, more responsive? Are you calmer? Is your blood pressure more consistently registering on a more normal level? Is your breathing shallow and stunted and in your chest or are you taking slower, deeper breaths, allowing your body to be fully oxygenated? Does your skin look dull and sallow, or are you told your eyes look bright and your skin radiant? Are you making better choices with your health? Are you more focused and productive? All of these are desirable and naturally begin to occur, maybe without you even noticing. However, your family, friends, neighbors, and coworkers will. Some of the changes are even more subtle, but I notice a more consistent and cumulative sense of well-being, replacing high-strung and short-tempered behaviors.

We don't judge what happens in meditation. The key is to surrender to what is, whether the mind is busy with unrelenting thoughts, or we go into the deepest stillness. It will change moment to moment and with each new meditation. It's what we do and how we act once we return to the activity of our daily lives, the beautiful chaos of life. Notice your thoughts now. I no longer get lost in those thoughts. If I notice I'm identifying with a thought, I ask, "Was I in the past or was I anticipating the future? Am I present?" It may be hard to imagine that your mind could slow down, but it cannot help but do so with a regular practice of meditation.

Meditation is meant to be effortless, but sometimes the ego cannot help being frustrated by the elusiveness of the gap. When chasing the high of it, it will remain just out of reach. Instead, we remember that the gap is not a destination or a trophy to acquire. It is always there, just beyond our thinking minds.

There's a former whaling town in the Western Cape in South Africa called Hermanus. I used to sit on the rocks of the cliff alongside the bay where I'd spend hours just mesmerized by the annual phenomenon of the whale migration in this quaint seaside village. Each year, traveling from the South Pole, the Southern Right Whales make their way to the bay of the small town to breed and feed their young, attracting local and international tourists, thrilling all who are blessed to witness the sensation of the best land-based whale watching in the world.

While whaling is now illegal in South Africa, Hermanus remains on the migration route of the whales, which can number upwards of several hundred at the height of the season. An occasional surprise visit from an orca was always a highlight. I learned a great lesson of detachment during the many times I sat watching the whales, getting lost in time and space, awestruck by these graceful behemoths. Breeching was a spectacular sight to behold, imagining that this animal was the size of ten elephants (about seventy tons!) and could catapult itself out of the water and into the air before plunging back into the sea. I wanted the perfect picture, the perfect video, only to find myself often disappointed as I'd lifted my camera for a good shot, but the whales would dive back down into the deep, leaving the water absolutely still. It was a moment of connectedness where I decided to stop worrying about taking the picture and resolve to just stay present in the moment. It's when I put my camera away that the real show on this particular day began. It's in the letting go, the surrendering to what is, where the magic resides.

The sky was perfectly clear and blue, and I sat on the cliff watching the bay. I got very excited when I spotted a mother and her baby and watched them for some time. I became concerned when I saw the mother swimming away from her baby and there was quite a distance between them now. How can you not be grateful for an experience of which I became a part? The mother flapped her fin once and from the distance came the baby's response as it slapped its fin. The mother hit the water twice with her fin and I held my breath as I thought, "Oh my God, I am watching her teach her baby." Sure enough, the baby slapped its fin twice against the water. This happened again with the mother slapping her fin three times. I just sat with my mouth agape, filled with awe and wonder as the baby responded with three slaps.

The ancient Chinese prophet Lao Tzu's first verse of *Tao de Ching* explains that the mystery will remain obscure as long as we are searching for it from outside ourselves. We must go to the source within to find the divinity in our own existence. Paramahansa Yogananda said, "The goal of yoga science is to calm the mind, that without distortion it may hear the infallible counsel of the Inner Voice." When we get quiet and listen, we will hear God, through physical sensations in our bodies, our thoughts, intuition, and clarity of vision, versus doubt and anxiety. Yogananda likens this to radio frequencies. When driving on a highway, the radio stations lose signal as you cross into a new county or border, so you reach for the dial, and scanning slowly going back and forth, you try to reduce or get rid of the static so the station will come in clearly. This is what meditation teaches us. Throughout the meditation, our thoughts will come and go, but when we become focused and calm, the static disturbances of our thinking will also become calm so God's frequency can come through. How do you know that it is God and not your ego? Use your body as a judge and ask yourself, "Does this feel comfortable?" We can only know the absolute truth when we ask the question, not with our five senses, or a focus on external rewards of some kind. Rather, we ask with awareness of our heart, which is the bridge between our physical body and our causal body or soul. From this depth of purity, there will never be doubt in God.

When we first learn, the experience of practicing meditation can often feel as if our mind is like a monkey brain, as described by Swami Vivekananda. "What can describe the uncontrollable restlessness of a monkey in this condition? The human mind! The human mind is like that monkey, incessantly active by its own nature; then it becomes drunk with the wine of selfish desires, thus increasing its turbulence." The observation of this alone can be very powerful as we begin the process of becoming the observer of our own thoughts. Dr. David Simon, co-founder of The Chopra Center, used to teach, "The thought, 'I was thinking' is the most important thought you will ever have." Thoughts become relentless; outer sensory input seems deafening; noises become louder; and sensations in the body can be frantic with nose itching, coughing, eye twitching. This restlessness is often a signal that stress is leaving the body. When these distractions calm down, the mind surrenders to the stillness and silence. These are all normal experiences during meditation. It may go in cycles, where you find yourself deep in meditation, not noticing time and/or space. Other times, the monkey brain reappears. or the body is agitated. I still experience too many thoughts. I fall asleep. I get distracted by noises. I recognize this as all part of meditation. I make an intention to detach, let go, surrender. These are not commands to rid my mind of all thoughts as that would just be futile. There is no forewarning of what the next thought will be, when it will arrive, and how or why.

Dr. Deepak Chopra, in an effort to provide a hint of understanding about presence, says, "Ask yourself, I wonder what my next thought will be." Nothing comes to mind. That "no-thing ness" is presence. It's the gap between our thoughts. It's pure existence. It's God. It's an intention to stay present with the meditation and not become attached to a particular experience, nor get focused on one thought. At some point during meditation, we may also become aware our mind has traversed a tangent of many. When we liken all of these experiences in meditation to waves of the ocean, we see how the wave builds up, rolls along, crashes at the shore, and then merges back into the ocean. We can do the same with our thoughts, and eventually the mind quiets down. Focus or not focused, we allow our thoughts to flow through and merge back into the space from where they came.

Living Yoga

The next time you get a chance to be by the sea or watch a video of the ocean, for a few moments, observe the waves as they come to the shore. You'll see that they don't hesitate or stop when they reach the shore. The waves aren't judging themselves or the other waves. "Wow, that wave is bigger than I ... How come that wave came in with such a rush and I petered on in?" Sounds silly, but don't we do this with our own thoughts? If we observe our thoughts in the same way that the waves come to the shore and easily, effortlessly merge back into the sea, we begin to witness how little power those thoughts can have on us. Without judgment, without attention, we allow our thoughts to merge back into the field of consciousness from where they emerged. Let them be what they're going to be. Let them go where they're going to go. They each have an energy as they push toward their potential. Each one is its own thing, what it's about to be. Without judgment, we enjoy it, each and every one. Yet, we put those artificial measurements upon ourselves.

The practice of meditation becomes less of a struggle against this whirlpool of thoughts (or *vrittis* in Sanskrit) and more of the practice of accessing the silence and serenity behind the thoughts. Within the framework known as the eight limbs of yoga are tools that help prepare the body and the mind for that stillness we find in meditation, such as *asanas* (postures or poses) and *pranayama* (breathing techniques that help to relax an active mind and calm the nervous system).

"In its calmness is found the greatest manifestations of power." This quote by Swami Vivekananda resonates with me deeply as I recall notes I wrote in a journal as a young adult. I wrote, "Solitude is my only refuge." Growing up in a large family, I've been blessed with lots of memories of togetherness, silliness, and fun. But as my mom once said to me, "You've always loved your silence." It wasn't so much a rejection of the tribe as a natural impulse to create the space to rediscover myself, amid the beautiful chaos of my family dynamic.

"That is what I mean by meditation—the Soul trying to stand upon itself." Meditation gave me the clarity to see that this has always been part of my journey—to stand upon myself, resting in the glory of my eternal spirit. In the words of one of my favorite poets William Blake, "If the doors of perception were cleansed, everything would appear to man as it is—infinite." That was meditation's gift to me, the revelation of the truth of my own infinity.

The promise of meditation, as written by Vivekananda is, "Then, the glory of the soul, undisturbed by the distractions of the mind or the motions of the body, will shine in full effulgence; and the Yogi will find himself as he is and as he always was, the Essence of Knowledge, the Immortal, the All-Pervading and Eternal Spirit." Paramahansa Yogananda described his guru to be in "a soundless state of breathlessness—a deep yogic joy." In a deep meditative state, the breath slows and in some cases stops as we transcend time and space and find *samadhi*.

"Medicines have limitations, the divine creative life force has none." Yogananda was able to experience spontaneous healing. This is not a new concept as all of the great religious texts speak of miracle healing. The medical community knows of it as the "placebo effect," or when the doctor says it's beyond medical understanding why this person is walking, seeing, alive, etc., it is called a miracle. When there seems to be no medical explanation, doctors declare the experience as spontaneous remission. Is it mind over matter? Or is it a great energetic force awakening and manifesting the inner healer that resides within all of us?

> You have seen how your health has exactly followed your subconscious expectations. Thought is a force, even as electricity or gravitation. The human mind is a spark of the almighty consciousness of god. I could show you that whatever your powerful mind believes very intensely would instantly come to pass. (Paramahansa Yogananda)

Yogananda makes a bold statement about how our thoughts affect our health. After many years of struggling with chronic nerve damage, going on and off pain medications, meditation and other yoga practices brought remarkable healing in my life. I was told that the nerve would never heal. I was told my body would experience withdrawal symptoms from the medicine. I was told I probably would never run or do yoga again after my surgery. All of these statements proved to be untrue as I deepened my meditation and yoga practices. The fear of chronic pain dissipated as I reveled in my returning health. I still experience pain occasionally. However, if the pain doesn't correlate to overexertion, I will examine whether I am lost in thoughts swirling around in my head that are steeped in the past. Or I check to see if I am fabricating scenarios of an illusory future.

In my yoga teacher training certification, I had a classmate who would stop anyone mid-conversation, including me, if they passed a negative comment about themselves or their expectations about life, reminding us that our thoughts have powerful energy. We never want to give the negativity any fuel. Dr. Wayne Dyer said the same in his PBS series when he said that we need to become conscious of everything that follows the thought, "I am." Televangelist and preacher Joel Osteen echoed Dyer's words when he said, "If you are playing the wrong 'I am' in your life, you are going to miss your destiny."

The ancient Vedic scripts say, *"Tat Tvam Asi* (I am that)." The Bible tells of Moses hearing God on the mountain saying, "I am that I am." These teachings all point to how the energy of our thoughts create our future. One thought I hold in my awareness each and every day is, "I am perfect health," which covers all the aspects of my multidimensional self: mind, body, spirit, and environment.

My experience with meditation changed the course of my life, and it continues to reward me with positive effects. Prior to making meditation a daily practice, I was stuck in life's melodramas, not knowing how to navigate all of the stories. In earlier years, I found myself suffering over these stories, but I was unaware of how to stop the madness. I once had a boyfriend who said to me, "Will it ever be enough? Will you ever be satisfied?" So for me, a yearning in search of greater meaning has always been with me. I didn't always look in the right direction or in the right places. And I certainly didn't always find it. However, when I did, I thought I had hit the jackpot! Searching outside of myself, I might have found the rush in some cool experiences, people, and material things, but that kind of hunt eventually led me to more searching, disappointment, or the emptiness of, "Now what?" or "Is that it?" Yoga, particularly my practice of meditation, has given me the insight to recognize the difference between happiness, which is often fleeting and unattainable, and joy, which is a reflection of the peace and contentment within. I still enjoy beautiful things. I still aspire to travel on my next adventure. I still have material desires, but now I'm no longer attached to them, nor do I wrap my self-worth or identity in the latest and greatest fad of the moment.

One of the benefits of meditation is the growing ability to release what no longer serves our higher good—the awareness, the realization of how destructive it becomes when we play that reel of the past over and over again in our minds or incessantly anticipate what has yet to occur, playing out scenarios that don't exist. There are moments in our lives that we do need to process, whether they leave us feeling elated or devastated. It's also prudent to have goals and to plan. And it's helpful to share our story, even cathartic to do a review and take the temperature of our lives. However, it's when we become so associated with the thoughts in our head, the stories we tell, or the events of our past or anxieties of the future, that we believe these make us who we really are.

There are times when I've been sad, angry, grieving loss. But what meditation has done is elevate my approach to life from ego to divine love. A couple of years ago, I would have also reacted from a constricted place. There are still times when I reflect back on a situation and consider what other options I might have had, which probably would have lessened my suffering. Meditation prepares me to respond, rather than react to the challenges I face.

When sadness emerges from the depths of my heart, the gift of self-awareness reminds me that I have a choice, to go into analysis paralysis, as my dear friend calls it, or step into gratitude and transform those less-than-pleasant, sometimes painful emotions into learning experiences.

I asked Roger Gabriel to explain further just how meditation affects karma. "Meditation is a powerful tool to transcend karma. Karma is affected by meditation because on a practical level, it rids us of stress, teaches us to be more harmonious, and balances the energetic force of our memories and desires, demonstrated by our thoughts, words, and actions."

Roger continued. "When we meditate with a mantra, we are using that mantra as a tool to transcend thought, journeying beyond our karma. The meaning of a thought holds the memory and desire and thus the karma. Primordial sound mantras have no meaning, so they have no karma. When you use your mantra silently in meditation, you are taken beyond the range of karma; you transcend all memories and desires and slip into the field of infinite possibilities."

When we have an association to a particular word, our minds will wander to that meaning. There have been students who have told me they didn't like their primordial sound mantra. More often than not, this was because the person was attaching a meaning to the sound or they had an association with something else. In this case, the mind wanders to that meaning. Whether pleasant or unpleasant is not the matter. As long as there is an association to a particular word, your mind will wander to that meaning. "And now you are just lost in your thoughts. That's very different from sitting with intention to meditate, using a mantra as a tool to allow your mind to come a single-pointed focus, diminishing distractions, allowing your mind to go beyond the field of memories and desires."

I am often confronted by how to navigate what seems like interrogation, fear tactics, and criticism about meditation, yoga, or my chosen path of spirituality. I understand it to be true fear on their part, fear that I am rejecting them—fear that controls their need to defend their point of view. I just want to have stimulating conversations where we ask questions that none of us can really answer. Even with the most devoutly indoctrinated religious sects, there is no way to know for sure what's really beyond, but we get to experience a sense of euphoria, bliss, and unboundedness when we transcend in our meditation and get a glimpse of the truth of our immortal, infinite, and unchanging souls.

When Jesus spoke of resurrection and everlasting life, is it possible his teachings might have been lost in translation, misconstrued, or interpreted to mean that only he was resurrected? For those steeped in their own religious belief system, this question might seem either blasphemous or absurd. But didn't Jesus mean we all have the ability within us to "rise above" through meditation? If we all have these experiences available to us, why do we waste so much time? It is the ability of our ego to fully embed us in the illusion of separateness. This is the veil (*maya* in Sanskrit) of which great teachers speak.

With a penchant for a better understanding, my conversations with Roger seem to gravitate toward the subject of *karma*, which generally opens the proverbial can of worms even among the most tenured scholars. Roger is always careful to remind me that the topic of karma has been debated, challenged, and written about for thousands of years, so it's unlikely we will find the definitive revelations over a lovely cup of ginger tea. But I continue my line of curious questions. If we believe that we are clearing our own karma with yoga, but our partner, family, friends, etc., have not or don't, I wondered if we can then transcend those relationships or do we also have to carry them into the next life? "It's possible, yes. But it depends on your choices and whether you are creating additional karma. If there is still some emotional charge or a sense of unfinished business, then there may still be an energetic connection still needing resolution." So, how do we know for sure? "We don't." Roger's response is not meant to be cynical. Even those sages we'd consider enlightened talk about how complicated the concept of karma can be. So rather than focusing on the weight of our karmic debt, we serve ourselves best in this life by practicing yoga through love and devotion (bhakti); action, work or selfless service (karma); wisdom and self-inquiry (jnana); or meditation and integrating the eight limbs of yoga (raja/the royal path).

There are many different meditation techniques, including those that use audible chanting, visual aids, movement, and those that are silent. Each has its value. I teach primordial sound meditation (PSM), an ancient silent meditation method revived by Drs. Deepak Chopra and David Simon, cofounders of the Chopra Center. Students of PSM receive a special mantra that is the sound or vibration the universe was making at the time of their birth. We use this mantra (which, in the ancient Sanskrit language, is translated as instrument of the mind) to go beyond our conditioned self. With focused attention on the repetition of the mantra, the meditator can move beyond the often turbulent, active mind to the field of pure consciousness, where the soul resides. This personal mantra is a silent tool or instrument to access inner calm, expanded awareness, and the truth of who they really are. As Deepak Chopra described more than two decades ago in his book *The Path to Love*, "This process of shifting from activity to stillness is a simple, yet very deep, description of meditation."

I wondered if the vibration of my primordial sound mantra is always the same, or does it change from life to life? As Roger further explained, "Our mantra is not the same because we come to each new life with a particular personality." The primordial sound mantra is based on your birth date, time, and place and calculated according to Vedic mathematics. Because the human mind, often fickle and erratic, has the tendency to be drawn out of silence, we continue to use the mantra in our meditation to take us in the direction of silence. There are many meditations where music is used, and they can be very relaxing and helpful in the reduction of stress. However, music, even if at a subtle level, keeps our minds active, drawing us outward with this sensory input, away from inward silence.

Roger's been meditating for more than four decades, and I've always seen him even-tempered in many different kinds of situations. So, I asked Roger if he ever loses his temper. "Yes. I've had moments where I've gotten upset, like with another driver on the road." What you must know about Roger is that he is one of the most serene individuals I know, and he emanates a glow that can only be described as pure love. So at least in my mind, when he says he gets "upset," it is unlikely Roger is referring to full-blown road rage. "But then I just laugh at myself." It's that practice of self-inquiry without judgment or criticism that brings calm and peace in all situations, a positive side effect of being a regular meditator. Even if the temper does flare, the rebound time and the suffering are minimized when we meditate. We are more easily able to cultivate authentic relationships and trust in the infinite possibilities of the universe.

When teaching meditation, the experience can be so powerful for some students that their eyes well up with tears, or others take a gasp of breath in remembrance, or a wave of peace has replaced apprehension or skepticism. It is an honor for me to be a witness to the connectedness, pure love, and gratitude that my students experience. With a regular practice of meditation, you no longer seek outside of yourself for validation. Truth becomes apparent. All thoughts, words, and actions stem from that center that is always available. I often tell my students that meditation and the practice of yoga is free. You don't need a prescription. You don't need brand-name leggings or a fancy studio to experience the benefits. It's already within you.

The catalyst for me attending an intensive, weeklong meditation retreat was to get away from the noise and to heal after surgeries. My intentions were to balance, nourish, heal, and transform and gently release all that no longer served me. My intention for healing was that it would be gentle because I felt strongly that what went in traumatically or painfully did not need to exit the same way. I had made that intention before an intensive Ayurvedic detoxification, a ten-day cleanse. And while others might have been experiencing their own tough process, there was a moment where I felt a swell of something wanting to be released. And rather than a wave of rage or sadness, or irritation and pain, I started giggling. I remembered intending to release things gently and knew that the laughter was my way of processing whatever was coming up. It reminded me of Mary Richards at the funeral of Chuckles the clown on *The Mary Tyler Moore Show*, where she also released her grief through uncontrollable laughter, which made me laugh even more. I had to excuse myself from the group so as not to appear insensitive to the delicate emotions and physical sensations others were experiencing. I laughed myself all the way to a hidden courtyard with beautifully manicured gardens and wrote in my journal, all the while aware of the lightness of being that permeated my cells.

When I teach meditation to first-timers, we go through the process of becoming still and silent. Typical responses will be coughing, fidgeting, incessant thinking, more bodily sensations, awareness, and attention on all environmental noise. After the initial short meditation, I will ask if the meditation felt comfortable, and more often than not, people will say how difficult it was to concentrate on the mantra when there was so much noise and activity outside. So I remind my students that it's not the silence outside for which we are looking. That's impossible to control. The silence we are intending to find is within. That silence is always there, always accessible, and always brings you back to your center, your ground state of being, which is calm, peaceful, in the flow with life's natural rhythms. That's why we come back reenergized on a nature walk, or we feel calmer after gazing up at the night sky. Nature is intelligent, doesn't resist change, and doesn't judge. It just flows with the universal laws. In meditation, we are accessing that same nature to which we are always connected.

When the waves come to the shore, they don't stop and judge

themselves or the other waves. They naturally go with the flow and merge back into the ocean. Your thoughts are very similar to these waves when you choose not to put your attention on them. You acknowledge the thought as it arises and witness it without judgment, without putting much attention on it. The thought fades away, along with the possible physical side effects of stress, anxiety, and other emotions. Like the waves of the ocean, the thoughts come and go. We can cultivate this skill of being the observer of our thoughts, without acting on them through a regular practice of meditation.

In my own silence, I feel a shift in perspective. When we attempt to know the unknown, we come from a jaded mind. There is no room for other possibilities or alternate and creative solutions. Trying to figure it all out based on past experiences only leads to "sameness." As Albert Einstein said, "No problem can be solved with the same level of consciousness that created it." However, when we rest in silence and move past the ego's need to control, we surrender to the unknown, to uncertainty. When we allow, when we trust, something better, something unimaginable is given the space to spring forth. Indian poet and Saint Mother Meera wrote, "In silence, more work can be done. The true experience of bliss is without words."

Living Yoga

Try this visualization exercise. Close your eyes. Take a few deep cleansing breaths. Allow your breath to come back to its natural rhythm. Place your attention on your heart, and breathe into that space. Now take a few moments to remember a special natural place you've visited, a beautiful waterfall, a gorgeous sunset, the memory of the exploration of an unknown forest trail, a terrific tropical storm, sitting by the ocean at dawn. It's your place, so choose the one you remember that made you feel connected. Continuing with your eyes closed, in your mind's eye, see the place and begin to activate the other senses—touch, hearing, and smell—and imagine any sensation associated with it. The purpose of the exercise is to demonstrate how these moments of quiet calm and connectedness to everything and everyone around us can also be a meditation. They are always available to use. We need only open a window on a crisp day and take a breath of fresh air; take our shoes off and put our toes in the grass; or look up at the night's stars or moon, etc. Or as we saw from this exercise, we can close our eyes and access those precious moments in our minds. We spend so much time replaying all the painful, disappointing, or stressful moments, creating negative effects on our physiology. So why not decide to replay all the pleasant, loving, and calming moments, reversing stress and cultivating positive effects for wholeness and well-being? Even the simple practice of gratitude improves our health.

The book *The 7 Spiritual Laws of Success*, written by Dr. Deepak Chopra, gave me a practical understanding of how to integrate these universal or natural laws into my life. The law of giving, for example, illustrates the circular exchange of the same energy of giving and receiving. I became aware of the difference between living from a place of trust and abundance, versus one of scarcity thinking and poverty consciousness. Today's Internet sensations or successful mentors, coaches, thought leaders, or other famous entrepreneurs reap the rewards of their confidence to value their talent, their time, and their products and services. Their success is tied into their belief system. On the opposite side of the spectrum are those with victim consciousness and a core belief of lack, a fear of not having, being, or doing enough. These individuals don't realize abundance in their lives because they don't trust or don't believe they are deserving. Fear of success or great wealth is also steeped in an expectation of failure.

When I was going to teach some friends meditation, I was told, "They can't afford to pay you. You should do it for free." There has to be an exchange of some kind to keep the energy moving, whether payment is in the form of money, the trade of products and services, or the donation of time or gratitude. This is the essence of the law of giving and receiving and the natural flow of the universe's abundance.

Since doing my first twenty-one-day meditation challenge and attending my first intensive meditation retreat, I had two major back surgeries and a rotator cuff repair surgery; became a Vedic Educator, certified to teach yoga, meditation and Ayurvedic Lifestyle; was challenged by religious zealots and faced many challenges. Yet, while having endured many life-altering experiences others might consider tragic, I feel elated most of the time these days. This is not to say that these challenges haven't been tough, and in some cases sad. However, I choose to find the blessing in each; I wake up each day with gratitude. Speaker, author, and life coach Bob Proctor teaches the exercise of waking up each day to this practice of gratitude. He suggests that upon awakening, list ten things for which you are grateful, list three people for whom you have conflict/tension and send them love, and sit quietly for five minutes and ask for direction for the day.

Chronic pain and chronic nerve damage was a lonely path. Even I would tire of talking about the pain. My least favorite question, which, to me, is subjective, is "On a scale of one to ten, how bad is your pain?" Well, the fact that it was a constant in my life during that time always made it a ten. Chronic pain wears you down. It can bring about depression. You isolate yourself because even the smallest tasks result in hours of elevated pain. And then there is disappointment when your loved ones ask, "Are you still in pain?" or "Are you in that much pain?" Rather than extending empathy, your suffering is seen as inconvenient or annoying.

Famed philosopher, speaker, and writer Jiddu Krishnamurti said, "To understand the immeasurable, the mind must be extraordinarily quiet, still." Roger Gabriel says that when your mind is quiet and you listen, you will hear God humming. Krishna tells Arjuna the same in The *Bhagavad Gita*, "For those who have ascended to yoga, the path is stillness and peace."

How do we do that when we are bombarded with the pace of social media and the effects it is having on our physiology? FOMO (fear of missing out) is now an entry in dictionaries, which is described as the anxiety one feels if one is not connected at all times to one's devices, scanning, trolling, creeping, or posting so as not to appear out of the loop of what's trending in today's pop culture. The suggestion to take some time to turn off and tune out of all the external noise that's invaded our thinking minds can cause great angst for some. But the practice of silence is actually meant to tune us into the real power, the power of the inner voice.

Technology has its place in the world, but being connected to the rest of the world through social media has only helped to disconnect people from themselves. With the constant barrage of messages and posts, we are always distracted and focused outside of ourselves. And the ego thrives on that mindless attention on external stimuli. If we are always only seeking answers from some external source, we've shut out our own creativity and inspiration and have replaced it with copying someone else's. The Vedas call it the veil. Fear or inability to be self-reflective for any length of time is easily covered up with mind-numbing behaviors and distractions.

Scientific studies on meditation are now revealing the healing benefits ancient yogis knew thousands of years ago. We now know that meditation reduces, and in many cases reverses, the ill effects that chronic stress has on the physical body. And now, recent studies are uncovering how the spiritual practices of silence, stillness, and meditation not only improve brain function, but a regular meditation practice also improves the quality of our lives, making us less reactive, more accepting, more joyful. It becomes easier to manifest desires and express creativity, not just in artistry and love, but also with ideas, solutions, relationships, and even finding more ways to have fun.

But some experiences that we consider negative, particularly when we first start meditating, may come to the forefront. Old wounds, old stress, or anger (old emotions) can resurface. However, meditation helps to work through this kind of stuff. While excavating the experiences that no longer serve us, we have a choice to re-live and replay them over and over in our minds or choose to become a witness of our lives, observing without judgment, learning to accept what is or what was. Meditation releases this kind of stress naturally with a regular practice, sometimes on a subtler level that we might not initially notice.

Chapter 6:10 of the *Bhagavad Gita* states, "Those who aspire to the state of yoga should seek the self in inner solitude through meditation." The rewards of practicing meditation, mindfulness, and/or silence are calm, stillness, peace, clarity, a sense of euphoria, and the physical benefit of the body's return to homeostasis.

I decided that I wanted to usher in my fiftieth birthday in absolute silence, which, for some, seemed odd, but I knew it would be the perfect gift. In the calmness and silence, there is power. These are moments where we can fine tune inherent qualities like intuition and clairvoyance. Silence is the breeding ground where seeds of intentions and desires are planted and nurtured into full bloom. It's the realm where creativity, new possibilities, new ways of thinking, and new ways of being are cultivated.

I would celebrate this milestone being present with myself, by myself, and for myself. I signed up for the Chopra Center's Silent Awakenings program, an advanced silent meditation retreat, where I'd be in absolute silence for five of the seven days, amid the serene setting of the Asilomar Conference Grounds along the Pacific Coast near Monterey, California. Asilomar was also the setting for Dr. Wayne Dyer's movie *The Shift*. The state park accommodations are simple and rustic, without television or other electronics in the rooms. I'd made a commitment to myself that I'd be off the grid for the week anyway, turning off my cell phone and leaving other devices at home.

Our group would enter complete silence the afternoon before

my birthday, and I made a conscious choice not to mention that to anyone. There was another sales/marketing group at the conference center at the time. They were not in silence, but Asilomar has hosted various silent groups, so the staff is well-equipped, especially during meals, when we would point and nod while our plates were filled as we moved along the cafeteria-style service. We had a separate dining room for our group, but prior to reaching the counter, the line included attendees of another conference.

There were a few people from the other group in front of me in line for lunch who were talking and joking. When they realized that no one else around them was speaking, it became awkward for them. You could tell by the increase in nervous chatter that this one guy, in particular, was very uncomfortable with the silence around him. He began making fun of us to his friend, but his female colleague looked uneasy and tried to deflect the conversation. I remember thinking how much louder everything seemed: voices, the clanging of dishes and utensils, clearing of throats, etc.

As I settled into the comfort of my inner journey, those sounds became muffled as a subtler sense of hearing became heightened. I was also aware of how my other senses sharpened too. In silence, I began to notice how my pulse mimicked that of nature and moments of clarity and profound calm now replaced racing thoughts about nothing. I could feel the roll of the ocean's waves through me; I woke up with the sun and went to bed with the rise of the moon. I took long walks on the boardwalk, allowing my senses to become more attuned to my surroundings. I sat by the giant fireplace staring into flames, feeling the warmth they generated, aware of the scent of the burning coals, listening to the popping and crackling of the wood and the hissing of the trapped water as it evaporated. I meditated at least twice a day, sometimes for extended periods. I joined other participants in twice-daily yoga classes that supported and nurtured us on our journey of silence.

Sitting with my back against one of the mature Monterey pine trees, I meditated and wrote in my journal. Sometimes I just sat silent, quiet, breathing in the scent of the pines, or looking out to the ocean. There was an open trail in the midst of these pines where I walked, trying to hear what my thoughts were saying, or I directed my attention toward the fauna and flora all around me and wondered what life would be like to surrender completely to the kind of trust, lack of judgment, and ease of flow the rest of nature has in its existence.

The group gathered to participate in a walking meditation along the boardwalk that took us beyond the famed Pebble Beach. I watched a lady playing catch with her black Labrador Retriever on the beach. I remember thinking to myself that this must be what living in the present moment is really like. Nothing else mattered to that dog but his owner and that tennis ball. He ran back and forth with intent, laser focus, and the sheer joy of life each time the woman whirled the plastic ball launcher, and I felt the same joy as I shared the experience from afar.

On another outing, I found myself laughing as I watched two squirrels playing. As they climbed on the barricade, chasing each other, I was delighted by the innocence, the folly of their games, and the purity of their being in the present moment. I remember thinking to myself that I felt like I was in an animated film as animals would approach and keep me company on the trails. Walking back to my room from an evening event, I came upon a mother deer and her fawn. I knew there were others from my group witnessing this too, but I tried to follow the suggestion of keeping the focus inward, not even making eye contact with other participants. We all stood there astonished as the mother deer appeared calm in our presence. Maybe it was because we were still and silent or maybe because, after a few days of silence, we were emitting a peaceful energy, but the trust in allowing us to be so close to her baby was definitely a gift. When we broke silence days later, my friend Liz and I related the experience with the same fervor.

At this silent retreat, I asked the question of myself, not my ego self, but my God-guided self, "What would you have me learn about silence?" Here's the insight I received during one of my meditations that week: "It's where your creativity lies. It is your truth. Life is effortless if you allow it to be so. Your vision is clear." I can promise you that I had never received this kind of advice when I went looking for answers outside of myself. The ego would have you believe that if you help me, encourage me, or congratulate me, somehow you will be left with less than I. When you are living yoga, you know this to be a fallacy. If you give abundantly with a pure heart, abundance will be returned to you in kind. As a primitive protection mechanism, the ego self also triggers us to be fearful. This instinct can be helpful in truly life-threatening situations, but the ego can also stunt our growth by paralyzing us with irrational fears. The true self guides us to trust, which is not easy when we are raised and conditioned to doubt our intuition, to fear the future, the unknown, and uncertainty. But any moment other than this one right now is unknown and uncertain. What if we do what the rest of nature does and just detach from the outcome and accept?

Acceptance of what is can only be accomplished if we create the space for pure potential to be nurtured. In silence, we access that trust, that truth, that power to create the life we truly desire, rather than trying to figure it all out, which only leads to sameness. When we attempt to know the unknowable, we come from a jaded mind. In the space of already formulated opinions, there is no room for other possibilities or alternate or creative solutions. However, when we rest in silence and move past the ego's need to control the outcome, we surrender to the unknown, to uncertainty. When we allow, when we go with the flow of life, giving up resistance and restriction, we open ourselves up to the boundless, the limitless realm of potential, we create the room for something better and something unimaginable to spring forth.

When silence is used against a person as a weapon of punishment, it can be torture for someone who believes he/she is the ego and the thinking mind. If our value and identity is contingent on approval from someone or something else, our self-image can often be shadowed by guilt, shame, and blame, or anger and hostility.

We are so conditioned to believe that we always need to be doing, going, and accomplishing that we feel strange, guilty, uncomfortable, ashamed, or even afraid to rest, to be still, to be silent. Everywhere and anyhow, we look for distractions and ways to escape, to avoid being alone with ourselves, with our own thoughts. Vivekananda says, "Meditation is the removal of attachment." The practice of meditation cultivates the pure silence that exists beyond our personalities and eventually conquers the ego's hold on us and our attachment to the relentless identification we have with our thinking mind.

The ego does not leave us willingly, nor does it dissolve easily without a fight. Our sense of self, our personalities feel threatened, but when we stick with the silence until those survival techniques of the ego, such as fear, doubt, and criticism, fall into the background, we find real peace. This peace is always there; it has always been there. We begin to understand that we always have access to it when we cultivate silence through practices like meditation and self-inquiry. And then we can use the power of the ego as an ally, rather than the ego using us, creating constant hindrances.

Dr. Deepak Chopra says, "Our individual egos have self-centered aims, tastes, desires, opinions, likes and dislikes. The very construct of the ego brings with it a built-in conflict with other egos." When we bring our ego, rather than open-heartedness, to a relationship, we find competition, comparison, conflict, and condemnation. Practicing the eight limbs of yoga loosens the ego's grip and instead, nourishes authenticity in our lives. A practice of silence creates space where creativity can then thrive.

Living Yoga

- Developing a practice of silence can start with the simple act of taking a few minutes before jumping out of bed upon waking, and before checking your devices, to take a few deep breaths, put your attention on your heart, and ask yourself, "What can I do to create a joyful day today for myself and for others?"

- Wake up a few minutes right before dawn and experience how nature ushers in a new day. Take in the brilliance of a sunrise.

- Winding down after a day of activity can be challenging, particularly now when we are all overloaded with external stimuli from one device or another and juggling packed schedules. That static can build up, leaving us hyper, irritable, impatient, fatigued, and burnt out. Try setting up a special space in your home, an environment that promotes silence and stillness.

- Nourish yourself with a bath at the end of the day with a few drops of natural lavender oil.

- Create the space and time to mindfully enjoy a relaxing cup of tea (without caffeine), or take your tea outside to sit and look up at the stars. Watch a sunset.

- Sit quietly and witness how nature marshals in the end of the day.

- Try adopting one day a week where you turn off the television, or your device, and have a meal in silence, remaining fully present to the action of eating. Experience the gift of nourishment with an acute awareness.

- Plan a walking meditation, a mindful practice made popular in the West by Vietnamese monk Thich Nhat Hanh. Walking in silence, become aware of each step. It's not in the destination or in the distance, but the awareness of your connection to nature as each foot is grounded into the earth.

- Take a few moments after your prayer ritual to remain in silence, allowing the seeds of your true intentions and desires to be planted.

FIVE

TRUTH AND AUTHENTICITY

> Unless one speaks the truth, one cannot find God, who is the soul of truth.
>
> —Ramakrishna

Author Mark Nepo wrote, "Still, the cost of not being who you are is, that while you are busy pleasing everyone around you, a precious part of you is dying inside; in this case, there will be internal conflict to deal with —the friction of being invisible." This quote struck me to my core as I worked toward being okay with knowing and more importantly, accepting that my words, however divinely guided I know them to be, may not be received well by everyone. This quote also resonated deeply as I knew this to be the case with critical moments and decisions in my life, where the risk to knowingly give up who I am is far more fatal than choosing the more acceptable, "normal" role, the one that always gains society's approval and acceptance. As artist Sia sings in "Bird Set Free," it was at the point where the whispers became screams, no longer able to be contained in the convention of it all, where one gives voice to that inner truth, regardless of the fallout.

I heard Oprah Winfrey tell Iraqi and women's activist Zainab

Salbi that she was a truth seeker, and I realized that I, too, am a truth seeker. As Patanjali taught in the *Yoga Sutras,* "When we are firmly established in truthfulness, action accomplishes its desired end." In my experience, truth is always there, even if only as a subtle knowing. For me, telling the truth has always come with much less suffering. Inspired by Gandhi, President Woodrow Wilson, in his own words, recanted his statements on violence and war, saying, "Let us now be in search of something new; let us try the force of love and God which is truth. When we have got that, we shall want nothing else."

It takes guts to ask for the truth, especially in the face of adversity, but it takes even more courage to accept it. And therein lies divine grace. As most people who have had transformative events in their lives, one of my greatest moments of truth came in the face of fear ... of what I might find out, what I might be told. Buddhist Monk Pema Chodron teaches that, "Fear is the feeling we experience as we get closer to the truth." And yet, I've also felt my strongest in asking the tough questions of myself as I knew my bravery would lead me to clarity, peace of mind, and triumph over indecision and melodrama. It brought me to my most authentic self, despite the sometimes unwanted or unexpected pain, sadness, and disappointment.

I was in my early thirties and enjoying the benefits of having climbed the corporate ladder. I wore the "right" clothes, now transported back to the sweet memory of the spectacular fit of an Italian-made suit as it draped over my body so perfectly. Taking the Los Angeles tunnel curve at 105mph in my Fjord gray 5 series BMW was another present moment elation that still makes me smile.

I noticed a new coworker in the hall. That first meeting felt more like the waves of a sonic boom passing through me. He was tall and handsome, and I felt an immediate connection. But I also remember thinking, "If he's not gay, I just met the man I'm going to marry." If we are paying attention, we will always get the truth in the way of some physical signal in our bodies. Often described as the only two real emotions, you either get a feeling of "yum" or "yuck." The key is to recognize it and more importantly, trust it. But our egos often rush in to protect us, and the rationalizing begins. "Oh, maybe I've just been in the television business too long," or "Maybe I'm becoming too jaded."

Robert and I enjoyed deep conversations, lots of silly moments, way too many diet sodas and gummy candies, but the friendship grew, as did the ambiguity of was he or wasn't he. There was a letter I had written to God asking for the truth. While all the nights out were fun—we got along splendidly and looked like an attractive power couple—I knew I needed to confront that tough question. I would be lying if I didn't admit that a part of me wanted to stay in the dark about the obvious question looming over my head, but the truth seeker in me knew I had to qualify what was really going on. In my letter asking for the truth, I also asked for the strength to accept the truth. That second prayer for strength of acceptance put love first before fear or any of the emotions the ego might have preferred.

Another nudge came from a gay coworker who had put me up at his place during one of my many housing transitions. After many conversations about this, my roommate and friend agreed that I needed to confront the ambiguity. He recommended I suggest a romantic movie for the next "date." When I walked in earlier than expected, my friend asked me, "Did he kiss you?" I told him we only hugged. He then asked, "Did you get the tap on the back?" Again, was it denial or naiveté? I wasn't sure. But my roommate looked at me and said, "No straight guy is going to see a romantic movie with you and then end the evening with a tap on the back."

For me, ambiguity left that evening, and I summoned up the courage to just ask. A long conversation in each other's arms followed soon thereafter. Nearly twenty years later, that tall, handsome, and yes, gay man Robert remains one of my best friends.

Why does it seem that standing in your truth is difficult or even impossible for so many? When does that urge to cover up, lie, dismiss, rationalize, "bend the truth," or embellish seem the better choice over our innate need for the truth? That impulse, desire, or act of deception does not come from our true self. Our ego, our own minds, take control through fear—fear of losing something we perceive as precious, fear of not having enough, fear of not being enough or that we might be left standing alone. Yes, you might be saying that's perfectly normal. For most of us, for a great portion of our lives, we use, often against our innate knowing or better judgment, some external measure as our reference point, or the attachment to or identification with our reactive, incessant thinking mind. The challenge with trusting these methods is pain and suffering that often come in the form of more fear, more egocentric choices, and more confusion as to why life isn't what it's supposed to be. Everyone else is doing it, wearing it, owning it. If your voice is different, that kind of tribal mentality wreaks havoc on your ego if you aren't aware and making choices based on external influences.

By always reliving or complaining about the past, we avoid living life in the now. In the same way, by only looking to the future to make things better, we don't take responsibility for our life today. In both scenarios, life has happened or will happen. We relinquish responsibility for our own lives or blame other people and circumstances when things aren't as we think they should be or anticipate how they have to be. It is nearly impossible to "wake" someone from this kind of sleep.

Personally, I suffered a great deal trying to "wake" loved ones. I was once told that I wouldn't get someone to hear by trying to stuff it down the person's throat. It felt like that sentence had the power to lift the heavy weight of trying to fix everyone right off my shoulders. That's exactly what I was trying to do, unsuccessfully, I might add. Something Gandhi is famous for quoting rang in my head all the time, "You must be the change you wish to see in this world."

The other famous quote that rang in my head, "Old habits die hard." I might have had the best intentions in the world to help, and I really did. I believed my intentions always came from a place of love. But it is an exercise in futility when the person you are wanting to help doesn't actually want your help. Or worse, that person didn't ask you to help. He or she just wanted to stand on the victim stage and reenact the melodrama. Without an internal shift or without a desire to truly heal from within, any guidance, advice, concern, or help I offered was not received well at all. Any attempt, however well-intended, would be rejected, resisted, or refused. Like the old saying goes, "You can lead a horse to water, but you can't make it drink." It took me a very long time and a great deal of fear and pain watching those I loved sabotage their own mental and physical health and their dreams before realizing they didn't want my help. I couldn't control their level of consciousness, no matter how well intended I might have been. As Frank Zappa wrote, "The mind is like a parachute. It doesn't work if it's not open."

Buddha expounded the benefits of detachment when he taught, "Well trained in the seven fields of Enlightenment, their senses disciplined and free from attachments, they live in freedom, full of light." Freedom for me came when I began to look at my own reasons for suffering. That internal shift made all the difference in the way I now show up for life. Trust and acceptance are the keys to understanding the law of detachment, as Dr. Deepak Chopra writes in his book *The Seven Spiritual Laws of Success*. "In detachment lies the wisdom of uncertainty … in the wisdom of uncertainty lies the freedom from our past, from the known, which is the prison of past conditioning." In this poignant statement, an echo of Buddha's teachings, I realized the natural flow of life is the permission to be and live free.

> Sooner or later, everyone will face not getting what they want. How we respond to this unavoidable moment determines how much peace or agitation we will have in our lives … for our acceptance of

> things as they are and not as we would have them allows us to find our place in the stream of life. (Mark Nepo, *Seven Thousand Ways to Listen: Staying Close to What Is Sacred*)

When we remain attached to our ideas of how we expect or want life to be, the fear of not being, not doing, or not having enough eventually turns us toward resistance and stubbornness in our thinking. The impulse to protect our fragile ego often shows up outwardly as cynicism and arrogance.

"Go then into the world and its battlefields, and amidst the roaring cannon and the dim of war. You will find yourself free and at peace." How can I write an honest book without sharing my journey? I'm here today as an author and teacher because of my choices, my circumstances, and how I chose to transform my world and continue to search for my truth. I made a commitment to come from a place of love and acceptance. It was no easy task for the ego to get on board with that concept, but I continued my own line of questioning. How did I get to this space? What are the gifts in these experiences? Who am I without society's acceptable labels?

What do you do when you encounter the gamut of reactions from family, friends, and colleagues when the transformation of your world becomes a reality? Mental health professionals call it "social mourning." There is a great deal of change that takes place during this type of evolution. "You've changed," is what I hear. The truth is I haven't changed at all. I'm more myself now than I've been in a long time. What did change is the world in which I choose to live. Mark Nepo says, as humans, we go through many transformations in a lifetime and says beautifully in the metaphor, "When a butterfly emerges from its cocoon, the cocoon wasn't false. It just served its purpose."

The news shocked many people to their core as my marriage seemed to represent the ideal partnership, and if ours could collapse, what chance did the rest of them stand? I understand the concept of this social mourning, so I was prepared for the fallout. But what you see as my failure is just a mirror of your own. With my yoga practices, I now see that I get to choose not to subscribe to the hysteria and melodrama within "the tribe." I was told, "Your acceptance of this is just odd." Maybe for others, but not for me. For me, the result of accepting life as it is continues to be more wonder, joy, spontaneity, and creativity. We are not meant to suffocate in a shell we've outgrown or one to which we subjugated our lives to appease others.

As a witness to my own life, I could see the options very clearly. I could make a choice that I knew was unhealthy for me in all realms, physical, mental, environmental, and spiritual. Or I could decide to honor me, knowing that I would be risking life as I knew it, but at the same time, protecting my own health, wellbeing, and security. I honored me, and all that I built crumbled. For those who know me best, standing in my own truth seemed the more obvious choice. For others, it was preposterous. How could I possibly even consider giving up a life of perceived material luxury for a life of uncertainty? The truth that those others can't see is that life is uncertain regardless of how much you try to anticipate, control, or cajole the future to be what you want, need, and expect.

A very dear friend of mine asked me recently if I thought my meditation practice and yoga studies have helped make my choices easier. Without a doubt, I can assure you that five years ago before I began a regular meditation practice, had I been faced with the trials of this past couple of years, my reaction would have been very different. I might never have questioned why my physical health was deteriorating. Sure, I could blame the oil company that extracted petroleum nonstop in our neighborhood. I could attribute the fatigue, headaches, and chronic joint pain to the cell towers that loomed over the homes in the neighborhood where I was living. However, meditation was starting to reap its rewards, one being a great sense of self-awareness. I wanted the truth, and if I wasn't going to get it from my partner in life, then as a truth seeker, I had to become my own advocate. As Glennon Doyle Melton says so beautifully, "If a woman has a choice between saving her soul and saving her marriage, she needs to save her soul." This salvation can apply to any commitment in life, any relationship, be it work, friendships, or family ties—the choice to deny your own truth, your own soul, can prove disastrous long term.

I have made a conscious choice to live in the space of love, not fear. So with love comes compassion, kindness, peace, calm, and acceptance. However, it's unfathomable for those who are not awake, who are fearful and reject any notion of meditation. I hear, "You need to pray," followed by what seems an awful lot like an interrogation of my religious practices. I choose not to engage in these conversations because they turn into monologues and soliloquies of dogma and doctrine. And no amount of debate, argument, or persuasion is going to bring acceptance or understanding of my experience. Nor is it necessary for me to try. Sure, you can read about meditation and quote books, including this one. But unless you meditate, you can't possibly reap its rewards or fully understand the experience about which I talk. It's like being an armchair traveler watching a documentary on Paris. Unless you have taken the riverboat cruise along the Seine River and crossed under the Eiffel Tower as the lights come on, you cannot possibly appreciate the magic of that moment. It remains as part of the intellectual database, but there is no experience attached to it.

In writing about my own personal story, the details of these most recent defeats and triumphs aren't as important as the healing process and my path to freedom. We are all connected by these circumstances, the patterns of archetypal storylines, the range of emotions we are all hardwired to shut down, hide, fear, dismiss, shame, guilt, or ignore. As children, many of us heard, "Don't cry. Put on a brave face. Don't tell anyone." Do these phrases ring true for you? Like I do, you probably have a few others you can add to the list. Told to us during our formative years, these kinds of statements shape how we deal with (or avoid) our emotions as adults, until we awaken to our own truth and authenticity. For me, it cracked open my heart and mind and left me with a peaceful levity that had temporarily disappeared amid my own ego's need to control the outcome. Like you, I have faced many challenges, traumas, and ups and downs throughout my life. The road that led to the writing of this book wasn't always pleasant, often disappointing, very painful, and sad but also deeply introspective and profoundly fulfilling and joyful.

It's not a learned skill to sit with the less-than-pretty emotions, such as suffering, sadness, anger, or disappointment. It is a practice to embrace the dark, or as Debbie Ford called it, the shadow. Spiritual leader Panache Desai speaks of welcoming the anger. Pema Chodron teaches a meditation of transforming emotions that are labeled as bad, negative, and dangerous or those that just make us feel too vulnerable. What we learn as we overcome our own stories is that emotions are just emotions. It's what we do with them, how we react to those emotions that determine whether we suffer or not. Anger, in and of itself, is not bad. It is the physical sensation of some deeper, hidden truth of hurt, sadness, disappointment, or fear. Rejecting, denying, or projecting them on others only serves to strengthen these emotions. If we recognize, acknowledge, and crazy as it sounds, welcome such feelings as anger, they then have the opportunity to rise up, like giant waves in the ocean, and if given the space, will subside right back from where they emerged. But we have to become aware of their rising to transform them, to allow these emotions to pass through without judgment, guilt, or shame. Those are the side effects of an unconscious reactive approach toward life. Yoga and its practices of meditation, pranayama, and asanas (poses—physical movement), among others, provide the tools to change how we choose to show up in our own lives. Actress Kerry Washington said, "I didn't have to be better. I didn't have to fix myself to go after the life I dreamed ... I started showing up for life."

The ambiguity in my life was once so painful for me. Probably unconsciously, I suppressed what I knew was in direct conflict with my pure nature. Mark Nepo says that courage is the heart's blossom. In my experience, I've seen emotional ailments manifest themselves in my physical body, and I've seen them manifested in the hearts of those who I loved. "Despite all consequences, there is an inevitable honoring of what is true, and at this deep level of inner voice, it is not a summoning of will, but a following of true knowing." To everyone in my life, the risk I would take was unfathomable. The pull toward the truth, embracing what I had always known, but allowed to be drowned in a pool, was immense and could no longer be denied. I knew the truth, but I literally left it there one day in a swimming pool, and I made a choice. No matter how noble my intention might have been, as I became more aware, I also became aware of how the consequences of that choice had been suffocating me. What seemed the obvious route, from a purely traditional perspective, turned out to leave me with an undercurrent of dis-ease, which eventually would rise to the surface. To be true was my only choice if I was going to come up and breathe again and live life fully.

As Sufi poet Rumi says, "That which is false troubles the heart, but truth brings joyous tranquility." Your true self knows only truth. So although for me, certain circumstances in my life were initially a shock and at times, very sad, I was intensely aware of the feeling that the falsehood of the life I was living would eventually extinguish my spirit completely if I allowed it any longer. I already knew it was squelching my true self. If a plant sits in a vessel that is too small for it to sprout, its growth will be stunted, and eventually, it will be suffocated by its own roots. Poet William Blake echoed my thought when he asked, "How can a bird that is born for joy, sit in a cage and sing?"

Even one more minute trying to drag out the truth, I knew, would be an ineffective and painful task for me. I finally recognized that the truth doesn't operate in the same reality for those with a low score in emotional integrity and there is little capacity for compassion, empathy, and pure love. For me to try and continually help someone come to a point of greater self-awareness was pointless, nor was it my job to do so. Self-awareness is either nonexistent or horribly distorted when emotional intelligence is lacking.

I honored my truth. In doing so, I knew I was going to risk shattering what was perceived, even by me, as the perfectly framed picture. But I was now awake, and so from a place of rediscovering the truth of who I am, the risk to look away or ignore the truth was way more terrifying to me. Going back to sleep just wasn't an option. And while the image splintered into a million pieces and brought with it a great deal of sorrow, my own heart expanded with joy and peace. I honored my spirit, my soul, my divine purpose. And with that insight also came the understanding of the blossoming lotus, which is described in yoga as the heart. The heart is the bridge between the ego and the spirit, and when those two are in alignment, the heart cannot help but go into full bloom. That is the essence of living a truly full life, and it is and has always been the promise of yoga. Following your heart's true desire is real freedom. It is what all the great sages have described as nirvana. The Beatles knew it when they sang, "All you need is love." Buddha knew it when he said, "If you meditate earnestly, pure in mind and kind in deeds, leading a disciplined life in harmony with the dharma, you will grow in glory."

Some of my favorite treasures I've pulled from my meditation practice include: a greater self-awareness; greater capacity for love and compassion; equanimity in the midst of adversity; softness of voice, while still being joyful, loud, and authentic; spontaneous right action; living my dharma; and truth and trust in the absolute.

What yoga has taught me is to detach. By practicing the law of detachment and not identifying with the emotions or thoughts that arise, they can then be more easily transformed. How often do we lose ourselves in our thoughts, either anticipating the future or replaying the past, rehashing the old stories or projecting unacknowledged wounds on others by creating new dramas, just to do yet another loop on that emotional rollercoaster? So how do we get off this ride?

If you get a chance, watch small, prepubescent children play. If a quarrel breaks out, they often resolve it easily (provided the adults don't interfere), and they go right back to playing, never bringing it up again. They live for that moment, and that moment only.

> People are taught from childhood that they are weak and sinners. The world is only made weaker and weaker each day by such teachings. Instead, teach them the truth! Teach them that they are all glorious children of immortality, even those who are the weakest in manifestation. Let positive, strong, helpful thoughts enter into their brains from their very childhood … Know the truth and practice the truth, and in time you will realize the Truth perfectly. The goal may be distant, but awake, arise, and stop not till the goal is reached. (Swami Vivekananda)

Vivekananda is urgent in his teaching. Unfortunately, we become jaded, hurt, and disappointed, abandoned, among other circumstances that shape our thinking. These wounds are often played out through lifetimes and passed down generation to generation until we learn the lessons, heal, and decide to choose differently, and blaze our own new trail. I honored my truth. And although treading an uncertain path can sometimes be painful and unsettling, I found peace in the wisdom of allowing, accepting, letting go. "Let go and let God."

While doing research for this book, I came upon a story of truth, strength, and courage that defies the actions of even the bravest of adults. Malala Yousafzai, Pakistani activist and youngest ever Nobel Peace Prize laureate, has become world-renowned for her global campaign for education for girls. At the age of fifteen,

Malala's defiance against the Taliban, demanding that girls receive an education, resulted in death threats against her and eventually an attempt on her life. She was shot in the head by a Taliban gunman. She not only survived but recovered with an even more definitive purpose for her life.

Words from Malala's speech at the United Nations were wise beyond her years.

> Dear Friends, on the 9th of October 2012, the Taliban shot me on the left side of my forehead. They shot my friends too. They thought that the bullets would silence us. But they failed. And then, out of that silence, came thousands of voices. The terrorists thought that they would change our aims and stop our ambitions but nothing changed in my life except this: Weakness, fear and hopelessness died. Strength, power and courage was born. I am the same Malala. My ambitions are the same. My hopes are the same. My dreams are the same.

When she won the Nobel Peace Prize and was invited to accept her award, she delayed the ceremony to receive her prize so she could finish her school day. She said, "How can I stand on the platform for education for all and then skip school?" To say Malala's bravery, determination, and capacity for forgiveness were admirable seems feeble in describing the demonstration of someone living with purpose and the flow of life, in yoga. All of life's intelligence conspired to make her vision a reality.

My former landlord in South Africa was a product of white privilege and the dictates of a government determined to control their own self-interests. He once asked me if I thought prejudice was a political motivation. I told him that to see differences is human nature, but to demonize, fear, discount, or shun is taught behavior and based on a collective ignorance. In excluding others because of their dissimilarities, we miss the richness of diversity in the experience of life. Vivekananda said, "We stand against our own spirit, against the majesty of God, whenever we refuse to obey the voice of our higher self." We see a bit of that in today's social media culture, where we not only don't obey the inner voice, but there is also so much peripheral noise, influence, and distraction that it's impossible for that voice to be heard. Too many people looking for external validation will mimic whatever latest trend they see. They may be unaware that they are squeezing out any potential to be a creative expression of their unique life in their attempt to feel acceptance from external sources. The need for this kind of external acceptance is at the polar opposite of what it means to be unified or in yoga.

"We have forgotten our potential." The endless possibilities are covered up by conditioned beliefs, competition, scarcity thinking. Creativity is squashed amid discouragement and lack of mental and physical space to manifest our unique expression of life. Our ideas are shot down; our imagination is toned down for being too loud, too weird, or too different. Our spark of creativity is snuffed out by our own and others' fear of failure. Too many originals were shunned, hidden, or shamed into silence. In this case, I mean oppression. Silencing your soul is just deadly, whether you agree to it or are forced into it.

Meditation, concentration, contemplation, reflection, and self-referral create space. I discussed this concept with my nephew, a budding singer/musician in New York. I could tell the difference between the music coming from Michael's soul and his heart and the stuff that was an attempt to clone the style that was popular at the time. I told him that great ideas come out of the stillness and silence within you. Otherwise individuality is mired by the "sameness" of the tribal mentality. That's why there are so many amazing bands and solo artists who are catapulted to stardom with their debut album, only to see their sophomoric release flop. It's because the first one was created from their authentic selves, deep passion, and love of the music. The second album, on the other hand, is either directed by the record label or created to appease them. True creativity doesn't fit into the already designed box.

Author Shawn Achor, former professor at Harvard University and one of the world's leading experts on the connection between happiness and success, quoted Paul's letter to the Romans in his favorite Bible passage from Romans 12:2 (KJV), "And, be not conformed to this world, but be ye transformed by the renewal of your mind." Teachings from the Vedas, Buddha, and Jesus, among other ancient texts and wisdom from spiritual sages, show us similar paths to do that. Meditation naturally brings you closer to your truth, so doing the "right" thing is no longer a question or a chore or a choice. Freely, you choose the right action.

The noise in your environment and in your mind (like worry) is deafening your path to meaning and gratitude. Spend some time in calm and quiet so what arises is your true purpose. Spiritual teacher Adyashanti wrote in *Falling into Grace*, "The keys to your happiness are no longer in somebody else's pocket from the past. They're in yours. And that's empowering."

The lesson for me, I think, is that I was the one, no one else, who sabotaged my own happiness. I devalued myself by giving up my boundaries to make others comfortable, second-guessing myself and putting everyone else first. I love the Eleanor Roosevelt quote, "No one can make you feel bad without your permission." There will always be someone thinner, prettier, wittier, stronger, more successful, but I'm learning that no one else can speak from my perspective or from my experience. When we deny our authentic expression of life, our creativity, we are denying the world the majesty of our creation ... and yes, we are all born with that majesty. I matter. You matter. My voice counts. Your voice counts. And I got the label "loud" because I was trying to persuade, convince, cajole, and command people to hear me. But the truth I suffered to remember throughout my life before yoga and meditation was that my true voice was what really mattered.

I was so busy complaining that I didn't belong; that no one was listening; or I was cowering to make others feel better about themselves. In doing that, I kept attracting or surrounding myself with people, jobs, and situations that gave me more of the same about what I was complaining. During those times, I wasn't respecting myself. I put everyone else first for fear of hurting, offending, and disappointing, and that's an awfully difficult place to be because there is no way out of that. It was when I began hearing my own inner voice that I realized that those jobs, those people, and those situations weren't in alignment with my values anyway. Someone will always be disappointed, hurt, offended, irritated, or shocked, but now with yoga as my compass, I am aware that I can only control my own behaviors, reactions, thoughts, words, and actions. And that self-awareness has brought me to a place where unpleasant situations are now evaporating from my daily life.

Harder than dealing with my own emotions has often been dealing with how others close to me react to my life situations. Expectations of how I should be acting or reacting are not being met. I haven't collapsed into bouts of depression, uncontrollable crying, fits of rage, or bad mouthing or gossip, all gifts of which I am fully aware and for which I credit my meditation and living yoga practices.

In search of my authenticity, I was led to meditation, and with this gift, I found a deep sense of knowing. The truth is that it's always been there. The internal whispers, if ignored, just became louder when I was quiet enough to listen. This was the golden key to my heart, not the one I expected someone else to have that would unlock my brilliance. Wow! I held that key all along. I just didn't remember. But when I did, I began showing up in my life differently. Native American elder, international human rights lawyer, advocate, and educator James Sa'k'ej Youngblood Henderson said, "To truly listen is to risk being changed forever." This time, I truly listened. I could now reach within rather than search for or expect others to hear my voice. And by the way, when I felt my external voice wasn't being heard, my ego was right there to make it more audible than I preferred, so much so that I was called loud, "chatty Kathy," and other labels I carried with me throughout my life. Up until that first experience with meditation, I didn't know any differently. But I now had a remarkably simple tool to access the ever-present authentic voice within me that needs no approval, appreciation, acceptance, or acknowledgment, except from myself. This realization was like peeling away a tough-crusted outer shell worn for everyone else's comfort, except my own. At some point, maybe because of expectations, conditioning, fear of retribution, criticism, or alienation, that outer shell became normal. Even as an adult, it was expected that I be a good little, quiet, pretty "girl." I wasn't little. I certainly wasn't quiet. I wasn't a girl. I was a successful international businesswoman and respected television professional running projects and companies overseas. So there was always something patronizing or condescending to call a strong, independent woman a girl, implying a helplessness that I didn't relate to within myself.

I heard throughout a great deal of my life that I was too loud ... and I now ask, according to who? In whose arena was I too loud? I also heard (and sometimes still hear) that I was too wild, too crazy, and too different. I think back to a child who I absolutely adored. She had that something, that sparkle of which stars are made. There was a moment in a diner when she turned to ask me what I would order for lunch. Yes, maybe her voice was a few octaves louder than what society said was "normal." She was put on meds. She was a child of a horrific tragedy, and expectedly so, she was very sad. So they put her on more meds. Yes, pharmaceuticals have their place. However, too often we are taught to suppress who we are for fear of embarrassing someone either too timid to live or asphyxiated by the opinions of others. In another story of a child who was considered "too loud," he, too, was put on medication. In his case, he did quiet down, but his mother noticed his personality had changed so drastically and she missed her real boy. She took him off the meds and found alternative ways to help him deal with his anxiety and behavioral issues. His creativity or his expression of life, which was labeled to be an over active imagination, blossomed. Mark Nepo says so beautifully, "Imagine if birds only sang when heard."

When someone tried to silence me, my external voice only got louder, while my inner voice time and again got squelched in favor of accommodating others' perceptions or comfort levels. And sometimes it still does, but now I can choose consciously, choose appropriately, and choose what serves me first. That's how you hold on to your integrity, your value, and your voice. Gandhi famously said that we need to be the change we want to see in the world. Change, however, can be alienating, for those who are doing the changing and for those who don't want the change. What if the changes, some obviously more visible, others more subtle, represent what people are either incapable of or unwilling to explore within themselves? This can make it feel like our spiritual path somehow is a judgment of their lives and often results in an undercurrent of anger bubbling to the surface and projected on to the one changing. But the option to go back to sleep once I was awake to this felt stifling to me. I felt trapped in the life of conformity I had created.

> For now, she not think of anybody. She could be herself, by herself, and that was what she now often felt the need of—to think; well, not even to think. To be silent; to be alone. All the being and the doing, expansive, glittering, vocal, evaporated; and one shrunk, with a sense of solemnity, to being oneself a wedge-shaped core of darkness, something invisible to others ... And the self, having shed its attachments was free for the strangest adventures. (Virginia Woolf, *To the Lighthouse*)

Even while writing this book, I struggled, almost paralyzingly so, knowing there would be a great deal of pushback as I transformed my world. But this time, it's not about whether others will agree. I can only come from a place of love and great trust that I am being divinely guided to share my experience in a way that provides you some insight toward finding your own key to transforming your life as well. Buddha was asked, "What have you gained from meditation?" He replied "Nothing! However, let me tell you what I have lost: anger, anxiety, depression, insecurity, fear of old age and death."

When I started doing Pilates and yoga many years ago, I always sensed that the aches and pains that would arise were old emotions getting shaken loose from deep within. The mantra at that time was always, "Thank you. Now, up and out!" Innately, I knew I could mobilize that old stagnant energy out of my body and my being and truly move on. I continue to be in tune with the signals of my body, whether it's in yoga class or off the mat. I've learned to pay attention to the aches and pains as messages of deeper insights. With meditation, I recognize the same process. Old conditioned beliefs that led to self-criticism, doubt, and fear needed to be mobilized. It is my belief that whatever needs to come up and out should be released gently as, for me, there is no longer a need to repeat or re-ingest the trauma or pain, whether physical, emotional, or spiritual. As Robbie Robertson sings in *Golden Feather*, "With a breath of kindness, throw the rest away." As Buddha taught, "In the end, only three things matter most: How much you loved; how gently you lived; and how gracefully you let go of the things not meant for you."

Mark Nepo wrote, "Seeking life everywhere I found it in the burn of my lungs." My own true voice I now shout from within, and what comes out is a softer expression of knowingness that comes from a place of love. I do, however, slip up, fall down, and get offended, and my ego will override my intention to remain in yoga. But that's the yin and the yang, the ups and the downs, the highs and the lows of life. Now, I often learn the lessons earlier. I recognize the emotions bubbling up and use my inner compass to see what's really going on and respond rather than react, always hearing my teacher's words, "There's no need to defend your viewpoint." But when those reactions happen and rear their unpleasantries, I acknowledge I could have done better and move on. In the past, I might have spent weeks suffering for past regressions because shame, manipulation, and guilt wreaked havoc on my mind as I wrestled with the repercussions of standing for what I believed to be true but was seen as rebellion against the status quo.

For me, it feels like the golden key to freedom, a breath of fresh air that says that I'm ok exactly where I am. I'm ok with exactly what I believe. I'm ok with what I need and how I need to express that, despite knowing criticism, judgment, sabotage, fear tactics, resistance, negativity and alienation may result. Maybe so, but to me the rewards of self-respect, authentic relationships, and being in the flow are on the other side, and they have the space with me to show up in my life. My transformation and its benefits are visible to even those who might condemn. It is done with love and grace, without the egoic need or desperation to defend my point of view or feel like I belong. In *The Path to Love*, Deepak Chopra writes, "To choose the sacred is to choose love." And that's all I'm trying to do. It's all I've ever tried to do. But too often, I submerged myself into conformity or became invisible because my voice was so different. For the longest time, I just didn't think I had a choice. Now I trust the inner knowing that says that we always have a choice.

"When you are full of joy, anything you intend or desire must be aligned with the divine." That to me is what Jesus meant when he said, "The kingdom of God is within you." We aren't here on this planet to be clones. We are here to each rejoice in our own unique expression of God, not anyone else's. Joy is a divine characteristic of the heart and when you follow your heart, you begin to see how the universal laws of nature work in the form of spontaneous right action. You choose what comes from the heart and the rest of the details are organized to help you succeed. When you ignore the heart's desire, what comes from that denial is pain and suffering, whether it's physical, emotional, or spiritual.

SIX

Living a Conscious Life with Expanded Awareness

The lotus flower, an important symbol in Vedanta philosophy, illustrates the human experience and transformation. The lotus grows up from the muck and into a beautiful multi-petaled flower, pristine without a speck of dirt. Much like our greatest challenges, our darkest hours, our greatest fears, we come up and out from the muck to reveal our pristine essential nature. As the poet Rumi wrote, "The wound is the place where the light enters you."

Dissolution or control over the ego might be our greatest challenge or suffering as part of the human experience. We do need the ego in our physical realm to survive. However, we can use the ego, rather than have the ego use us. We can learn to use our memories, rather than letting our memories use us. What can we do when we are confronted with challenges and/or suffering?

Dr. Deepak Chopra teaches a self-awareness technique called STOP:

S—Stop
T—Take a breath
O—Observe
P—Proceed with caution

I don't believe that we voluntarily engage in adversarial relationships. However, we know that the accumulation of past experiences leave impressions upon us, which can lead to knee-jerk (or unconscious) reactions and other not-so-pretty behaviors. The result of those behaviors is what really causes us to suffer. You might be thinking, "Well, that person is just nasty to me." Maybe so, but when you use Dr. Chopra's STOP technique, alternative outcomes become possible.

In the instance where you know someone is nasty to you, make a conscious choice to no longer engage at all, becoming unavailable to that person's negativity. If that's not possible, let's say it's a coworker with whom you have to complete a project, in this person's presence, STOP and take a breath. This allows you to come to be present in the moment, maybe even put conditioned beliefs about this person on the back burner. Observe. Without analyzing or judging, simply witness what's going on. In the moment that you take a breath, you actually notice the person appears really sad to you. You have just shifted your presence of being from ego where you are guarded and judgmental to one of love where you experience compassion. Proceed with caution. You ask this person, "Are you okay?"

Remember that you can only control your own behavior. There is no telling whether this person will break down and share with you why he/she is sad or bark back with, "None of your business." If we take one breath and say in our hearts, *I am open to the idea that there are other possibilities, that I have a choice,* even when you might not believe it to be so, you are sending out a welcome notice for all possibilities, all choices to present themselves to you. I had this happen to me recently, where I greeted a colleague. His response was short and dismissive, which was out of character for this normally friendly guy. Later that day, he apologized for his reaction, explaining that he was very sad as he'd just gotten notice that his job was being dissolved. How often do we make assumptions and get offended? By not taking this behavior personally, instead, I was able to extend friendship and compassion.

When someone asks for my guidance, my opinion, or my advice, I now ask, "Are you asking me to tell you what you need to hear or what you want or expect to hear?" The responses will be different depending on their intention to be open or their willingness or inability to do so. If you already know the answer or have been conditioned to believe it one way, then you have closed the door to anything different. And different isn't always to be feared.

So when someone says to me, "I have no choice," or "That will never happen," my reply is now, "You are right," or "That's true." Our thoughts create our reality. If you don't like your reality, create a different one. Choose differently. Even the slightest shift toward acceptance can catapult you forward to a more pleasant present.

In a conversation with someone who has the intent to be open or is more self-aware, the response is something more on the lines of, "Hmm, I never thought about it that way before." Can you feel the opening up, the expansion in that phrase? It's the creation of space, the allowing of a new viewpoint, not right or wrong, not better or worse, just new or different. This is where the potential for growth and change occurs. It doesn't happen in "I have no choice."

Living Yoga

Take a moment to feel this statement in your body: "I have no choice." There's a constriction, a tightness, a rigidity, a closing up or shutting down. Here, there is no space for growth, no room for change, and yes, you are left with no choice.

Now take a moment and feel this sentence in your body:

"Anything is possible," or "I am open to possibilities," or "What if?" Now maybe you just took a big inhale, feeling your lungs expand and your chest open. Or maybe you simply felt a bit calmer. As Dr. Deepak Chopra says, "Depending on how constricted or expanded our consciousness is, our reality shifts."

When we reside in a perpetual state of constriction, resistance, and rigidity, we don't evolve. We cannot expand our awareness, and we limit ourselves from the magical wonders of life. In that narrow place, we develop blockages, not only in our physical bodies, but on a more subtle level in our mind, intellect, and ego. These blockages show up as impatience, irritation, cynicism, judgment and criticism, physical pain, restlessness, insomnia, and other ailments that ultimately lead to disease.

Alternatively, with an expanded level of consciousness, we are able to invite other possibilities into all areas of our lives. What a welcomed gift to know we always have a choice. We can mobilize this stagnant energy, such as physical, emotional, and environmental toxins, old traumas and current stress triggers to allow for new energy to enter and bring in new life and fresh *prana*.

The tribal mentality, or the powerful collective consciousness, can wreak havoc on one's inner guidance system if it differs from the majority. I grew up in a family the size of a small tribe, which didn't leave much space or time for individuality. In searching for that individuality, my own voice was often not the popular view; or it challenged the status quo, which often had me exiled to the Island of Misfit Toys. Part of accepting my individuality was learning to be okay with being the misfit. I wasn't trying to be different or rebellious; I was just trying to find my own expression of truth. As a child, I loved the animated film *Rudolph, the Red-nosed Reindeer*, and I adored the scene where Santa Claus accepted all of the toys on the Island of Misfit Toys. Regardless of how different or weird, they, too, deserved to make a child happy, to fulfill their life's purpose, and to serve humanity.

Complete surrender of our personalities, our identities, and our conditioned beliefs can be very difficult in a society where people have become overly identified by their egos (positions and possessions). In this state of consciousness, there won't be much willingness to take this journey because what else is there if we don't have ourselves? The answer is we have our true selves, the infinite spirit that is divine! Siddharth Pico Raghavan Iyer, known as Pico Iyer, a British-born essayist and novelist, told Oprah Winfrey on her *Super Soul Sunday* series that he had this dream of selling all of his possessions and moving to a Buddhist temple in Japan, which he did. He tells of how, while he was there for a short time, he realized and said, "This is a lot of work." That path wasn't necessarily suited for him, but he did say he lives a sparse life with his wife in a small home in Japan, which was vastly different from the posh, fast-paced, stressed lifestyle in which he was previously engaged.

"No one becomes purer and purer; it is only a matter of greater manifestation of the perfection that has always been within. The veil drops away; and the native purity of the Eternal Soul begins to manifest itself. Everything is ours already —infinite purity, freedom, love and power." Somewhere along the line, someone or something led you to believe otherwise. The veil Swami Vivekananda speaks of is our ego, the layers and layers of conditioning we inherited or adopted or to which we submitted, consciously or unconsciously.

"For the one who is in you is greater than the one who is in this world." Here is where Jesus speaks of the soul versus the ego. When we seek to put the law of detachment into effect, we are surrendering our attachment, our identification with those objects of our desires or the chains of our fears. Of course, we can all appreciate beautiful things; we'd all like to enjoy life's luxuries. These are subjective and transient, as our ideas of beauty and luxury are a matter of either personal taste or personal conditions (social, economic, cultural), and they are always changing. A Masai chief in Kenya has no use for the latest and greatest snow blower, and a prized cow doesn't hold much currency in an upscale suburban neighborhood in the United States. Begrudging someone else's physical or natural wealth is just a reflection of our own attachment to the ego-based reality. When we measure ourselves and others against external assets, titles, or personas, suffering creeps in, and we blame our lack of happiness on outside influences because we are coming from a place of lack and scarcity rather than real wealth and abundance. "From your balanced life, they will understand that liberation is dependent on inner rather than outer renunciations." Yogananda wasn't suggesting that you shouldn't acquire and enjoy material abundance, but the detachment from your ego's sense of self and identity, which is often wrapped up in these positions and possessions, reaps a balanced life.

It's when we remember and embrace who we are at our core and what we are meant to do in our lives that the true majesty and mystery of life reveals itself. It's like the scene in the film when Neo realizes he is "the One" and the matrix crumbles right before his eyes, never to be rebuilt. Once you've awakened to the truth of who you really are, the illusion will crumble too, and it will be impossible to avoid the bliss and joy that comes from this deep knowing. That awakening begins with asking the right questions of yourself. Who am I? What am I doing here?

That's why we hear this story over and over again: "I woke up one day years later not knowing how I got here." This reflects how we are sometimes unconscious, just going through the robotic motions of the day to day, mindlessly following society's current expectations of what success, happiness, and a fulfilling life are supposed to look like. And when you are different or at a disadvantage, somehow that is perceived by the "tribe" as lacking or inferior.

Playing over and over in our minds are a loop of memories like old movies, and we feel the effects of rehashed emotions in our mental and physical wellbeing. The past doesn't exist, so why is it that so many of us are controlled by it? We live in a constant state of reactivity—our emotions dictating our behaviors. Equally detrimental is thinking about or anticipating the future. It doesn't exist either, and yet we incessantly create stories in our minds of what might happen, crafting the what-ifs in our minds, with many opting for medication for illnesses, such as anxiety, hypertension, or depression induced by stress and worry. The past and the future don't exist, but we ruminate over nonstop storytelling of how we think it should be or might be or should have been or might have been, leading us only to stagnation. Once you craft a story about the future or replay one from the past, you've closed the door to pure potential. Creativity, possibility, adventure, and surprise all live in the present moment and that silent space between our thoughts. Dr. Deepak Chopra in *The Third Jesus: The Christ We Cannot Ignore* so eloquently describes the present moment as having the qualities of alertness, openness, freshness, innocence, spontaneity, fearlessness, replenishing. "Radical uncertainty is at work all the time." Yet we spend so much time complaining about what's already taken place or trying to control what is yet to be created.

Living Yoga

We can explore ways to reach that divine consciousness that is God by practicing truth, trust, and gratitude. Remember an experience where your ego disappeared and you felt your heart expand. Maybe it was the exhilarating accomplishment of reaching the summit of a mountain. Nothing else exists in the present moment of the birth of your first child. Devoted lovers can experience God through a sexual experience when it moves beyond only the physical and the two are connected spiritually and energetically as one. In a similar way, whirling dervishes lose their ego in a sacred ritual meant to lose the ego and connect to the divine energy. Maybe you experience this sense of unity through great music you wrote or a piece of art you appreciate or one you created. Is it in cooking a beautiful meal for your family?

Become aware of those moments that feel precious to you, where spontaneous love just flows.

Rainn Wilson, actor and creator of Soul Pancake says, "There is no difference between art and prayer. It's an offering of yourself, your truest self." Your truest self can be revealed while listening to a piece of music or writing a piece of music that moves you and moves through you. While getting lost in the stroke of your paint brush as you create, manifesting something from nothing, your truest self is painted on the canvas. On that blank canvas of our lives, nothing is really the potential for anything.

A dancer's fluid movements are a physical and energetic expression of her or his true self. And when it comes from the heart, what is created is presented with a knowingness that he/she is part of the air and space in which the dancer moves. When you experience someone who lives with great passion for his or her *dharma* or purpose, you witness someone reaching his or her highest potential, which is the truest expression of God. This was apparent as I interviewed a friend about his great love for surfing.

A true Southern California surfer dude, Bob was dressed in board shorts, a surfer logo baseball cap, and a T-shirt and eager to talk about the sport or as he describes it "more like a religion." He was quick to rephrase so as not to offend, but I knew exactly what he meant as I've often described rock concerts like religious experiences ... being at a U2 concert, where it felt like Bono was singing directly to me. And, at one point I thought he was as I was close enough to catch a few beads of his sweat as I was swaying back and forth singing every word to every song at the Joshua Tree Tour. That kind of experience still generates the same emotional charge for me now as it gave my twenty-one-year old self in the moments it happened.

It is obvious the experience of surfing is more than just a sport for Bob. When I asked at what age he started surfing, Bob recalled his earliest memory as a four-year old on a surf board with his father, another devoted surfer. Within seconds of standing up on the board, the little boy wiped out and was under the water, and as his father tells the story, was quickly pulled up by his hair. Bob says he doesn't remember exactly how he got out of the water, but he does remember being terrified and running back to the sand swearing he was done with surfing. But the lure was too strong, and as a tween, he took up competitive body boarding and eventually moved to stand-up surfing. Bob quotes the surf company Billabong's slogan, "Only a surfer knows the feeling" as we begin talking about his draw to the ocean and his love and passion for surfing.

What we both discovered in our conversation that day was how much surfing was a metaphor for life and the euphoria that accompanies those moments when you are in the flow, in yoga. Even in the ocean, there are unwritten laws and when followed, not resisted, denied or challenged, the rewards bring about an inexplicable bliss. True surfers, as Bob calls them, know the rules, like "the guy or girl closest to the peak gets first priority," and if there is more than one person in the same position, they can agree to "split the peak," where they can each take the wave only if they go in opposite directions. The metaphor continued as Bob described his experience of surfing on the North Shore in Oahu, a spot considered to have some of the best surf in the world, as "bigger waves of consequences." So, like the safety precautions, laws and courtesies in a car on a highway, surfers follow the guidelines and respect the elements at work in nature to avoid mishaps, injuries, and even death.

Like the benefits of attending a yoga class, surfing has its physical benefits for the body, and Bob told me it reverses his bad habits of sitting at a desk all day. While hunched over the computer with shoulders rolled inward and the neck strained all day can leave one's body very constricted, surfing does the opposite, with the chest and shoulders expanded up and out with proper form. There is a great deal of physical work in the whole process of surfing, from preparing, putting on the wet suit, waxing the board, paddling back and forth, to getting up on the board and riding the wave to shore. Wiping out sounds like a great deal more work to me as the body is pummeled into the crashing waves as the surfer must regroup in an instant. As with yoga and as with life, when you put in the hard work, when you are passionate about what you are doing and you have a willingness to navigate changing conditions, you develop flexibility, endurance, and strength.

"Surfing centers me." Recently, Bob said he found himself really wrapped up in the political race, getting irritated and angry, "But then I go out in the water and all of that goes away." We continued to talk about how surfing, to him, is a meditation or mindfulness practice and what mental benefits he gains. "It's coolest to be in the barrel. All surfers want to live life in the tube." Surrounded by nature, the wind is blowing. He hears the sound of the rushing water. He tastes the salt on his mouth, and with all the adrenaline coursing through his veins, an overwhelming sense of calm permeates his entire being.

I knew the kind of experience he was describing, much like being "in the gap" in meditation—the suspension of time and space, connectedness, being one with everything. It sounded more like a master class from a wise teacher, rather than a cool surfer dude. I could see he was also aware of the insight as he continued. "It's incredible how time and all circumstances are conspiring for me at that exact moment for that exact wave. They're all different. I've never ridden the same wave twice." Holding his hand at his heart, deeply introspective, Bob was trying to give words to something that cannot be created, intellectualized, but only experienced, "It's hard to explain. It gets really quiet. All the peripheral sounds go away, and all you hear is the water. Your focus gets very sharp as your only concern is getting out.

"Gliding on a wave transcends everything. My board is an extension of me, and we are an extension of the ocean. We are coexisting, and for me, that's when it becomes therapeutic."

I said to him, "Bob, you've just described the essence of what it means to be in yoga, in union." We are that already. It's moments like that when we remember. That's why they are so powerful. This is the dichotomy of life where there is calm, serenity, and spaciousness, and at the same time, exhilaration, wonder, and danger. The characteristics of our hearts, not our egos, are what, when cultivated regularly, hold the keys to a balanced, contented, and fulfilling life.

Briefly we talked about looking into his daughter's eyes when she was born. Babies are just a bundle of pure potential, pure love, pure God. Again his hand reached up to his heart and he smiled and said "Hard to explain." He poignantly illustrated what I've described in this book about the difference between having the experience versus trying to intellectualize the unworldly, our divinity, and the presence of God.

The difference between a good wave and a bad wave is, just like life, a matter of perspective. A messy day, as Bob calls it, can bring frustration where your ego goes "hunting for the wave. It becomes an adventure, an expedition." I asked him to consider what's in the energy of the intent. Are you approaching the upcoming waves with frustration and an ego need to accomplish or with excitement and adventure and possibilities of just accepting whatever transpires? "It's a puzzle I like to solve, examining wind conditions, different waves, where they break, etc." He agreed that if you just make the space to allow, the puzzle unfolds before you as opposed to forcing the pieces together. Bob adopted his father's motto, which is, "Always make the last wave your best wave." Those kinds of positive expectations open the door for pure potential, unfolding surprises, often unimaginable to our limited egos. So it's not a question of good or bad but how you show up—how you deal with the fluctuating conditions. On his way out of the ocean on this particular day, another surfer asked, "How was it? Should I bother to go out?"

Bob responded, "Even the worst day surfing is better than sitting on the couch."

Bob's young daughter had joined us outside at a good moment to end our conversation as the sun had begun to set with a beautiful Encinitas, California, sky as the backdrop. She was proud to tell me that she was learning to surf and was a junior lifeguard. I knew she was also taking dance lessons and decided to ask her to describe her experience dancing. At first she responded from her head, saying, "I make sure I'm doing my best, and thinking about following all the steps."

I asked her, "So after you know all the steps and you stop thinking, then what does it feel like?"

She curled her hand upward, twirling around, and with a smile said, "It's like being up in the clouds." Bob's daughter had just described the experience of yoga.

> Because man himself is an expression of the Creative Word, sound exercises on him a potent and immediate effect. Great religious music of the East and the West bestows joy on man because it causes a temporary vibratory awakening of one of his occult spinal centers. In those blissful moments a dim memory comes to him of his divine origin.
> (Paramahansa Yogananda, *Autobiography of a Yogi*)

Just as communing with nature brings a source of inexpressible peace and unity, we also feel the healing benefits of music, even if we cannot seem to put into words the effects it has. Even when we are unaware, the vibrations of sound, including our spoken words, have tremendous power. A few decades later, I still vividly remember me and my friends describing the experience of our first rock concert as a religious experience. It might have been that we were praying our hearing would come back after standing near a giant speaker all night; but we could feel the energy flowing through us. It was exhilarating. That sense of aliveness, connectedness, love, and joy is the very essence of yoga, where the ego disappears and all are one in the same experience.

Studies have shown the mechanics of sound waves on the physical body too. In physical therapy, we use ultrasound to break up blockages and buildup of scar tissue or to increase blood flow to areas to effect healing. But sound can also have damaging effects on our health. It may be a code in our survival DNA that recognizes it as unpleasant, but just mentioning fingernails on a chalkboard has a visceral reaction for most people. I mention this because it is crucial for our wellbeing to become aware of what we are ingesting through our five senses on a daily basis from our environment.

Living Yoga

Not everyone is inclined to have meditation music or classical music on their playlists, but the next time you are listening to something on the radio or streaming app, pay attention to the lyrics and the melody and see if you can identify how it is affecting your physical body, your emotional state, or your behavior. Are the lyrics filled with violence? Do you feel a bit more stressed or irritated afterward? Do you notice that your heart is racing, and not in that exhilarating flashback memory way, but you feel less patient later on in the day; you find your road rage is amped up; or you feel unsettled in your gut and even realize that your burrito has now caused you some uncomfortable heartburn?

A small shift in that playlist to something more relaxing or less aggressive in traffic can have an effect on your mood, behavior, and physical or emotional health. For me, if I have a headache, oddly enough, sometimes turning up the volume of a guitar solo from my favorite rock anthems is very healing. Other times, it's an ice pack on my head with the sound of the ocean waves. So, for this exercise, become aware of what sounds you allow into your environment. Sometimes we have little or no control of what music or ancillary sounds to which we are exposed, but when appropriate or possible, we can make choices that will resonate on a more pleasant frequency for us.

Buddha taught, "Our life is shaped by our mind; we become what we think. Joy follows a pure thought like a shadow that never leaves." In the same way, an evil thought or intent can only reap evil and suffering. As we cannot govern the behaviors of others, the practices of yoga direct the questions inward, allowing us to develop greater discipline over our minds, rather than our minds controlling us.

Living Yoga

In an exercise in self-reflection and contemplation, consider what possession or position, title, or role with which you most identify. If any of this is taken from you, will you still be you? We hear the same story again and again about fame and fortune, seeking it, only to discover that it didn't bring happiness after all; or it was thrust upon an unprepared person, but what was found was more misery than the expectations of happiness. This exercise is really about detachment, letting go of what it represents for your ego self. You don't have to sell all of your possessions and go live in a monastery (unless you are inclined to do so), but think of something that has great value for you. Would you feel joy to share it or give it to someone else or would you lose sleep over it and be filled with resentment?

With self-reflection and attentiveness to our own thoughts, we can ask of ourselves: How am I living with divine direction today? Am I speaking, thinking, and acting from a place of love? When the answer is yes, there is peace, calm, and clarity. If the answer is uncertain or no, and we choose to proceed anyway, the results are usually fear, anxiety, pain, and suffering. And what follows is guilt, shame, regret, worry, indecisiveness, blame, criticism, and victim consciousness.

My intention is to practice more often the limb of yoga called *pratyahara*, which means gaining mastery over external influences. The particular influence I describe here, however, dates back to very pleasant memories visiting with my grandmother as a child. I love ice cream … good ice cream. Roger Gabriel once said to me, "So you can have the ice cream any time you want, but you don't need to ingest the calories." I was new to the deeper teachings of yoga, so I thought he was making a joke I didn't understand. Logically, I know the fat and sugar combination is a deadly one. I've also discovered that the origin of the genetically modified ingredients in my favorite ice creams at the time were making my joints hurt. I knew I would feel achy for several days after indulging in my frozen delight. So why did I do it? Because according to my ego, sometimes only reflecting on the sensation of the sweet, smooth, cold treat just doesn't satisfy my craving. Pratyahara helps to cultivate a discipline of the five senses, delaying or deterring instant gratification of my outer senses. It is in this place of awareness where I am better able to make more wholesome choices for my life. Other times, I fully indulge my pleasure senses and serve up my favorite vice, still enjoying it with mindfulness.

During a recent visit to my mother's home, I was surprised as much as my mom when my sister and brother also decided to surprise my mom for her eightieth birthday celebration weekend. After dinner one evening, I learned I was not the only one with a deep passion for the frozen gold! We all served ourselves and sat at the table together to eat our ice cream.

One person said, "Oh boy, I shouldn't eat this."

Another chimed in, "I'll have to work out at the gym twice as hard tomorrow."

In that moment, I decided to speak up. "Whoa! Hold on!" Everyone got quiet. I continued, "Please don't say those things. I don't eat my ice cream with guilt." And I saw the light bulb go on for each one of them as I said, "If I'm going to enjoy my favorite dessert, I only eat it with joy. Guilt or shame are two toppings that I choose not to digest with my ice cream. I sit relaxed, not rushed, and I savor each and every delectable sensation."

Everyone agreed that it was a good policy and, there was a shift in their experience from one of "Oh, I shouldn't," to "Mmms" and "Aahs."

Since writing about this particular experience on the topic of ice cream, I've learned that one of my favorite brands now has several non-GMO flavors, and once again, I make informed choices. So how is it that I am writing a book about yoga and talking about ice cream? It's another real-life situation where I can be aware of my actions and practice karma yoga in my own health. By choosing a higher quality, albeit more expensive ice cream, rather than mindlessly choosing the chemically riddled options, I can fully relish my experience and know that the following day my joints won't ache.

There is a wonderful lesson I teach in the Perfect Health Ayurvedic Lifestyle® course about mindful eating. I use this ice cream example to illustrate how our emotions can affect the way we digest our food, along with our life experiences. Again, it is the practice of self-awareness. If I can take one moment before and ask myself, "Do I really want this ice cream?" The answer is usually yes. But if I've had a stressful day, eaten a heavy meal, or know I am going to be rushed or distracted, then the answer will be no.

> The same creative force that generated the universe created your body. It is vibrating with intelligence and spirit. It is ultimately sacred and worthy of your love, respect and intention. Take good care of it and it will take good care of you. (Dr. David Simon)

Dr. David Simon wrote about the innate intelligence we possess to heal ourselves in *The Wisdom of Healing: A Natural Mind Body Program for Optimal Wellness*. And this is another way yoga has impacted my life. Most of the choices I now make for my body are made in the presence of these types of self-reflective questions. How will this make me feel? Is this a nourishing choice for me right now? From this space, we can truly be our best and act in the best way for ourselves. When we respect and honor our bodies, we are in yoga.

Living Yoga

These questions can be asked with any situation in life. Try reflecting on some of these questions before your next meal. When it is time to decide on what to order on the menu or what to grab from the pantry or fridge, ask yourself one or all of these questions: Am I really hungry, or am I just tired or angry? Will it be the most nourishing choice for me to eat while I'm stressed? How will this make me feel afterward? If you know there will be self-imposed consequences, maybe choose differently.

"In the long run, we are all sure to join the ocean of life and bliss." So the question is, do you want to flow freely and consciously or aimlessly about? Do you want to continue blaming life on other people, situations, or things? Or will you choose yoga as your compass and live joyously, creating a life beyond your wildest dreams, seeing the divine in everything including the challenges, mishaps, and disappointments? That's the promise of a life of bliss about which Vivekananda spoke. With yoga, you will accept all of life with calm, peace, and joy. Even the greatest challenges, tragedies, and disappointments can be turned into a miraculous life so long as we keep accepting, learning, and moving forward. Life is meant to be experienced in the present, not the past or the future. It may seem odd to hear someone say, "Getting cancer saved my life."

But the awareness of how something as scary as cancer could have a blessing in it is when the shift takes place. Our lives are filled with similar stories of strife and hardship that bring powerful personal growth and transformation. We also expand our hearts to be less self-absorbed and more loving and compassionate toward others as we also recognize their pain.

When the clouds cover the sun or the blue skies, we still know they are there. It's the same with our soul when the layers of conditioning, our personalities, possessions, roles, and titles, form a layer over the infinite reality and conceal the truth. There is a deeper knowing that our soul still exists behind all of the muck. "Our work, therefore, is not to make the soul free, but to get rid of the bondages." Vivekananda uses the metaphor of bondage to illustrate a similar sheath that hides our own soul, but it doesn't negate its constant presence.

We need only examine the mental, emotional, physical, and spiritual imbalances in our lives to recognize that our bodies are only reflecting back to us hidden truths, our deepest emotions, buried traumas, hurts, and disappointments that we either suppress or we don't have the emotional intelligence to process them. These chronic behaviors, habits, and choices lead to physical manifestations known as dis-ease.

When my friend was living in a highly toxic environment, she'd describe her life, and it did seem horrific, a situation with which I wouldn't be willing to live. In an effort to ease her pain, I'd offer advice, alternative ideas, new ways of looking at things, and each time, my friend dismissed what I suggested. I finally said to her, "Let me throw this sentence out there for you ... what if there were other possibilities?" And therein lies the question and the answer to life's suffering. If we just took a moment to be silent, meditate, reflect, contemplate, pray, whatever term you want to use to open your mind, calm the torrent of thoughts, we'd tap into the field of all possibilities, our own innate wisdom, intuition, and truth.

I quoted to my friend, "One day, you will just be sick and tired of being sick and tired."

In the sludge of her frustration, anger, hopelessness, defiance, and defenses, there were statements being made where I recognized that this highly intelligent, hard-working professional, devoted mother, daughter, sibling, friend, was waking to her truth. In the darkest of her moments, I saw the illusion being shattered and a fiercer, more confident, and authentic being emerging.

By entertaining the thought of other possibilities, my friend cracked opened just enough space for a creative solution to present itself. Whether she believed it to be true or not, didn't matter. What did matter was the mere fact that she had the thought, "What if?" In that question is an innate trust in, as Deepak Chopra refers so eloquently to it, the wisdom of uncertainty. What was certain, what was already known, was that the current behavior and approach to dealing with this life challenge *always* got the same results, which included knockdown, drag-out fights, disrespect on both sides, rage, disappointment, etc. My friend blew through that mental roadblock, and the path to peace and resolution became attainable. Her willingness to detach from certain material possessions also yielded her being awarded them all!

Stories like this might sound familiar. You went on vacation and got pregnant after years of trying and being told it was impossible. You began volunteering instead of obsessing about finding a mate, and someone far beyond your imagination showed up. The name of a friend, who you haven't seen for way too long, pops into your head at the exact moment that person phones you. You've heard the expression, "There are no such things as coincidences." When we live a conscious life, we are in harmony with the universal rhythms and trust divine intelligence. We make choices from a more awakened state, and our life begins to unfold in unexpected, surprisingly better ways than we imagined.

How do you get comfortable with living in uncertainty in a world that bombards you with fear conditioning?

At the time, I was living in Santa Monica, California, and referred to it as my soul place. I was well aware of my good fortune for having secured a rent-controlled apartment three blocks from the ocean where several of my favorite palm trees stood at the entrance to the building. I surely hit the lottery with two parking spots, which was nearly unheard of in a popular and crowded beach town.

My weekday mornings often began with a six-mile walk along the bike trail to the border of Venice beach and back up to Montana Avenue for coffee and the best white chocolate and apricot scone at my favorite quaint cafe. I had several friends in the neighborhood who were formidable walking partners, including Rhonda who I called my drill sergeant. There was one morning where I woke up to the sound of palm trees thrashing about as the Santa Ana winds had arrived. It was a feeble attempt to use that as an excuse to bail, but I tried as I exclaimed, "It's really windy out there!" My friend replied, "Are you going to blow away? Get up, I'll be outside your apartment in 10 minutes." She hung up the phone before my rebuttal and I jumped out of bed and readied myself for the morning hike. I complained that I really didn't want to go walking this particular morning, but soldiered on as Rhonda kept up her role as sergeant. When we finished, we realized that in my attempt to get it over with, we had transformed my complaining into a more positive energy that allowed us to shave 15 minutes off our usual time.

While working as a public relations consultant and freelance writer in Los Angeles, I thoroughly enjoyed the autonomy of creating my own schedule and the freedom from the traditional office grind. The myth I often debunked with my peers who were required to clock in at 9am was that I was living a life of leisure. The truth was that I often worked way more productive hours than they did because I had fewer distractions to interrupt me. I also worked late in the evening to accommodate overseas clients.

I remember one of my former co-workers got snarky upon

hearing that I'd taken an afternoon nap during a weekday. I told her that by 9am, when she was just arriving to her desk, I'd walked six miles, did my daily routine, completed a conference call with an overseas client and joined another client for a breakfast meeting. So, yes, by 3pm, I'd put in a full day's work and was ready for a quick power nap.

Working as a consultant had it's benefits, but could also be unsettling in the leaner times where a check in the mail wasn't always guaranteed. I didn't know that I was practicing yoga at the time when, intuitively, rather than focusing on the worry or becoming desperate in my attempts to secure more work, I used the space in between projects to nourish my creativity, to re-connect with nature and trust.

We hear it all the time that there are no such things as coincidences. Synchronistic events are always happening, ultimately for our higher good, even when we are unaware. I rounded up my industry contact list and began the annual task of sending out holiday cards. I didn't give it another thought once I'd dropped the stack of mail at the post office. It was less than a week later that I received a call from a former colleague who said synchronicity must have played a part in our re-connecting. He'd been frustrated with his lack of success in searching for a PR Director when, at the exact moment, my card arrived on his desk.

I initially turned down this job offer as I didn't want to re-enter the corporate environment. I explained that I'd be willing to work as a consultant for him, but he was very persuasive in convincing me to take the staff position. A little more than a year into the job, and multiple business plan detours later, it became obvious to me that the stability of the company was in jeopardy.

For vacation that year, I signed up for a fitness retreat to Kona on the West coast of Hawaii Island (known as the big island). I didn't know it at the time, but that trip would be the catalyst for another crucial point in my life and my career.

The retreat was set up by my chiropractor Yoshi, who was also trained in acupuncture, martial arts and yoga. Accommodations were at his estate on the island, where coffee, mangos and macadamia nuts grew. While most of the guests were there just to enjoy their vacation, I was on a personal quest. Each morning, we set out early for a new challenge and each evening ended with watching the sunset, either enjoying some of Yoshi's family recipes or grilling outdoors on the beach or in the lush forests on the island. Yoga classes and jogs up the sand dunes on the beach were tough, but I was in Hawaii to get some clarity in my life, so I loved every grueling minute of it. It never dawned on me while I did a two-mile swim in the ocean that there might be sharks in the water. I did, however, delight in a visit from the protected sea turtle, observing the regulations against touching or getting too close to it.

That evening on the beach was imprinted in my mind as one of the more memorable sunsets I've been blessed to witness. I marveled at how, no matter which direction I turned to look, nature painted the sky in spectacular palettes.

We spent time at a secluded self-catering establishment in the valley where wild horses came to hang out with us. We hiked up into the forest and crossed rivers on foot. We camped out among the stars and slept out on the beach to catch the rising sun.

An excursion to the famed South Point cliffs would mark the beginning of a new journey for me. We were told of the legend of South Point that said when you jump off the cliff, Hawaii's goddess Pele would take all of your troubles away and when you climbed back up, you would be renewed. That sounded glorious to me! There were two spots to jump. The main spot had the height greater than that of a five-story building and landed you in the swirling waves of the ocean. The other jump was into a natural-made pool and was much shorter.

I wasted no time in walking to the edge of the cliff. Before the rest of the crew arrived, I instructed the guide to count to three and I jumped! I remember thinking how shocked I was at the speed in which I was plummeting toward the sea with my belly now in my throat. I hadn't stopped to get directions on how to properly jump off a cliff so I landed in a seated position with the force of being thrown out of a window onto solid concrete. As my body was submerged, adrenaline raced through my veins as I screamed one very strong expletive out loud in the cold water as I pushed myself back up to the surface. Fear was non-existent as I realized I was alive, I could still move my toes and fingers, so I hadn't broken my spine or any other bones and I couldn't have felt more exhilarated. I swam to the iron ladder nailed into the rock face and realized I now had to climb straight up the side of the cliff.

What I didn't know was that everyone at the top was peering over in disbelief that I had actually done it. The guide knew I jumped incorrectly, so he jumped in afterward and swam toward me. By that point, I had already started to ascend the rock. When he asked if I wanted help, I turned and said, "Back off, I'm doing this alone!"

When I reached the top, I couldn't tell if my chiropractor was terrified or proud of what I had just done. He asked, "What did you do?" And my first response was, "I decided that I'm going to quit my job." By the time we took photos to commemorate the moment, the backs of my legs had swelled and were black and purple. The plan was to head to the green and black sand beaches for an afternoon hike, but everyone wanted to take me back to the house. I refused. Instead, I sat on ice chunks from the cooler all the way to the beaches and proceeded to spend the next 3 hours hiking. When we returned that evening, the Ukrainian housekeeper was so concerned that she felt compelled to nurse my legs with ice packs. I was grateful for her care and I assured her it looked worse than it felt. To this day, I believe that it was the best decision to do that hike and keep the circulation moving in my body. I wore those bruises as a badge of honor for having the courage to conquer South Point. I honored Pele for her protection and for the clarity for which I had been searching. Years later when I'd travel back to

Hawaii for a meditation retreat, I made sure to acknowledge Pele again.

I made the decision to part ways with that company because their mission was no longer aligned with my own values. Many of my colleagues, including the co-founders didn't believe that I was leaving my secure job to venture into the unknown. I didn't have another job lined up and I had no idea what my next step would be. I just knew that I trusted the message I received that day at South Point.

There were moments that weren't comfortable at all, wondering if I'd find a new job or go back to freelancing. I understood this space of unease as being in limbo and I practiced being ok with it. I wasn't aware that I was practicing detachment. As Deepak Chopra writes, "In detachment, lies the wisdom of uncertainty." I now know it to be yoga, the practice of accepting what is, staying present in the moment. There was a shift for me from limbo, which, for me, came with fear, to this wisdom of uncertainty, which rests in love.

But during that uncomfortable time, I was looking for some sign, some acknowledgement that I would be okay if I trusted myself, this deeper inner knowing that made me sense things would be fine. About two months after leaving my job, my ego was getting the better of me and my trust was teetering. As part of my usual morning routine, I walked to my favorite cafe and I ordered my coffee. I walked to the back of the cafe to grab a stirrer and some napkins, all the while deep in thought. I only noticed a woman standing next to me at the moment she leaned in to whisper, "You have nothing to worry about. You are protected." It was as if she was responding to my thoughts, but how could she possibly know what I was thinking? I hadn't spoken my thoughts out loud. I smiled and thanked her. But it still seemed odd to me, so I turned to capture another glimpse of the woman. It was even more of a surprise when I saw there was no one there.

I walked out of the cafe and there in front of me was a crisp hundred dollar bill. I knew instantly, beyond a shadow of a doubt, that the woman had been there to deliver a divine message. Finding that hundred bucks was confirmation.

Nowadays, if those moments of uncertainty are steeped in any fear, I remember that hundred dollar bill and trust that all is well.

Roger Gabriel says, "We are all on a spiritual journey toward remembering our true nature. We are not here to try and get Enlightened. We are Enlightened. We just need to remember." Some of us have brought memories of God's pure love with us throughout our lives. Others devote their lives to God. Others have some traumatic or pivotal experience that jolts them into memory of their divinity.

In my conversations with Roger Gabriel, I asked him to talk to me about karma, to clarify the meaning for Westerners who generally use the term to mean something bad. The translation of the Sanskrit term *karma* is action. The universal law states that for every action, there is a reaction; for every cause, there is an effect (the law of causality). For every choice, there is a consequence. It doesn't mean the consequence or reaction has to be catastrophic, but everything in the universe is made up of energy and any action, including the choices we make in our lives, leads to that energy being put into motion.

When we are born, we bring with us a particular karmic debt that our soul intends to experience, work through, and wash away during a particular lifetime. Karma itself is neutral but is made up of what Deepak Chopra calls the software of the soul. We have memories and desires that can affect our actions, and based on our choices, we either clear certain karma or create more. We live our lives based on that karma unfolding and following the formula or natural law that we must repay the energy. Some tangible examples of karma might be the toxins and stress we have that prevent us from living a happy and fulfilling life. When we are not in alignment with our pure nature or following our true dharma or purpose in life, we create more stress, more suffering. Karma and dharma are closely connected. Gandhi spoke of this when he said, "The perfect state is reached only when the mind, body and speech are in proper coordination. Every problem would lend itself to solution if we determined to make the law of truth and non-violence the law of life."

This again speaks to the current education system. We spend all of our formative years studying science, history, mathematics, and the like, but use the word *spirit* in the classroom and you could have a lawsuit on your hands. Professor, author, and Buddhist Jack Kornfield speaks about his Ivy League education in this same fashion. He says, "I only received half of an education. I learned sciences, history and mathematics, but nobody taught me how to deal with my fear or my anger ... the emotional stuff, which is what plays out in our lives." He is spot on! Budgets for the arts have been drastically cut, in many schools in the United States even removed all together for lack of or redistribution of funds, or legislation that denies the funding altogether. No longer do the students have the quiet space to create, to recharge, rejuvenate, relax, and use their imagination. Have we really become a society where music, art, photography, and poetry have become "fluff"? I might not have liked Mrs. Horn's teaching style in music class, but I grew to have a deep appreciation for the classics and those moments where we sat listening to a piece like the "1812 Overture" are forever implanted in my memory. Art class was a chance for me to explore the dark side of my art, where painting blood on the Doors album cover design may have been seen as morbid to most, but my art teacher allowed the expression without judgment. The now archaic process of developing film to reveal what I saw in the camera's lens was what I'd now describe as Zen-like. There was no instant gratification like Snapchat. You remained in the present moment allowing the process to develop and unfold.

"People with well-developed emotional skills are also more likely to be content and effective in their lives, mastering the habits of mind that foster their own productivity; people who cannot marshal some control over their emotional life fight inner battles that sabotage their ability for focused work and clear thought." Daniel Goleman's statement is being backed up by studies now on the effects of excessive use of our "smart devices." Studies show that, while individuals may score high on intellectual scales, these same people who lack enough face-to-face human interaction are becoming socially inept, detached, or indifferent. While these devices provide countless conveniences, the hazards are also many, including the rise in anxiety-based disorders and hypertension.

I have been vocal in the past about my opinion regarding the policy of everyone getting a trophy. To me, where is the lesson of sportsmanship and grace in both winning and losing? When I was a student, regardless of whether you were upset at the loss or not, the entire team on the losing side would go to each member of the winning team, shake their hand, and congratulate them. The winning team celebrated but didn't gloat. They enjoyed their win for sure, but they accepted the losing team's handshake with grace and congratulated them for a fair and well-played game.

If all we need to do is stomp our feet and throw a temper tantrum or post a rant on social media to get what we want, where is the grace in accepting life's challenges? Where are the lessons in compassion, gratitude, or acceptance with grace? Are our children being taught how to identify and cope with feelings? Who is guiding adults as they are confronted with big losses, pain, fear, and disappointment? Unless you actively participate in your own emotional health, you may not even recognize that complaining has become a bad habit and you've either gotten used to the suffering and agonize alone or you're deep in the trenches of victim consciousness and wear the suffering as a badge. Or you stuff it down and rage against society. Jack Kornfield is referring to the other half of education, learning the attributes of living a life with an elevated spiritual awareness. These include: kindness, gratitude, humbleness, honor, integrity, and compassion in diversity, rather than hate, fear, and divisiveness.

Meditation presents that direct experience to the practitioner and allows you to distinguish between the thought in your mind from the one witnessing the thought. How can you know to what I am referring unless you have your own experience? You don't even need to know, but being in yoga means you practice non-judgment, accepting without necessarily agreeing, but also not dismissing it or challenging its validity, just allowing. Your way is valid, and my way is no less valid. Allowing things to be as they are just means you are not willing to suffer in the name of being right or making the other person wrong. That is the practice of yoga.

Living Yoga

The next time someone shares a personal story with you, try practicing the art of real listening. Without interjecting with opinions, advice, or challenges, be present and just listen. Become aware when your mind has drifted to what your response will be. Give this person your true attention. Real listening takes some practice, but eventually, you will see the gift in being fully present for the other person.

When you are confronted with an unexpected turn of events, see if you can engage in the practice of allowing, accepting without judgment the people, things, or circumstances you cannot control or change.

SEVEN

GOD AND YOGA

Today, we can certainly use more acceptance, compassion, and tolerance when we speak of the diversity of our belief systems. "Small-minded people take one of these subdivisions and take their stand on it, and they not only deny the right of every person to interpret the universe according to his or her own light, but dare to say that others are entirely wrong, and they alone are right." Although to me, Vivekananda's use of the phrase "small minded" seemed judgmental, the meaning might have been lost in translation. Less aware or operating on a different realm of consciousness may be a better description for those who would waste time, energy and love to battle another's chosen path. Mark Nepo wrote in *7,000 Ways to Listen*, "Once we admit that we're not sure where life is taking us, then we are ripe for transformation."

I remember thinking, "How can I write a book about yoga without mentioning God?" I struggled with how to broach this as we become fiercely protective of our faith, our religion, and our "tribe" in comparison to others. But when I speak of God, I am not pointing to doctrine or dogma. I am referring in this book to pure love, recognizing the divine in everything and everyone. The path of yoga is the path to pure love—the only true path to God. As Dr.

Deepak Chopra says in *The Seven Spiritual Laws of Yoga*, "You will discover that God is not difficult to find. God is impossible to avoid, for there is nowhere that God is not."

The deeper aspects of all religions express the same goal to find greater meaning and truth. We see that in the form of community, prayer, ritual, worship, devotion, meditation, scriptural study, and selfless service. So rather than focus on the differences of each religion, which cast all others aside as "wrong," when we open our hearts, we see each religion ultimately has the same goal: to know God. The ancient texts known as the Vedas unify all belief systems in their teachings pointing out that we ultimately all want the same thing.

Many ancient seers used the metaphor that all rivers run into the same ocean to describe the goal of all religions to reach God. Chinese philosopher Lao Tzu wrote about it in *Tao de Ching*. It was written in Ecclesiastes. In the *Bhagavad Gita*, Krishna says, "All paths, Arjuna, lead to me." In an article written by Swami Tyagananda entitled, "Religion vs. Spirituality," Tyagananda wrote, "Religion paves the way to freedom. Spirituality carries us across it. Without religion, there would be no road, without spirituality, there would be no force to take us across." Religion's impact and its effect on people become an individual experience. I fought so hard to get it. We know God through the direct personal experience within.

Every Sunday, religiously I would attend mass. I wanted to feel its power, but I often sat bored or irritated at the obvious agenda in the sermon. And then other times, a priest's words would resonate, and I'd feel the charge of the spirit within me. In longing for peace, I'd sit in the pew, not understanding that I was meditating, but I'd be transported to that place beyond time and space, oblivious to the ceremony or ritual going on around me. Whether it was the beginning of a hymn, the congregation standing, or a bell, some distraction would catapult me back to the local realm. That direct connection to God, that very personal experience, was and still is indescribable and cannot be understood from an intellectual level. It is the place of truth, clarity, wisdom, and knowing.

Decades later when I was taught the mechanics of meditation, I instantly recognized those moments in my life. They are not and cannot be fully explained intellectually. Meditation makes that search for God that is somewhere outside of myself sheer folly. I know without a shadow of a doubt that my relationship with God is a celebration of the divine within me. It is from this place alone that I can then recognize the divinity in everyone and everything. This is why yoga has become my compass.

That "place" wasn't a place at all, but the non-local field of pure existence, a deeper sense of being that transcended the local realm of time and space, direct access to God. Here is where I experienced truth and clarity, only I didn't have the words to articulate my experience because I wasn't taught how to express it. The idea that you could reach God from within your own being wasn't something the church was going to freely divulge to its congregation. So, I, like many people who've experienced higher states of consciousness or a state of awareness of absolute truth and clarity, were silenced, dismissed, or chastised for voicing this knowing.

A friend shared with me the story of an experience he had as a child. It sounded similar to the kind of experience I described above. In a moment of silence or deep contemplation or even daydreaming, one can slip into what is referred to as "the gap." Because there was nothing in his catechism classes that might have explained what happened and no priest or teacher ever discussed anything like this during Sunday sermons, my friend had no knowledge with which to gauge what he experienced. He described it as being very silent, very dark, and peaceful. However, when he emerged from the gap, the thoughts his mind was accustomed to took over in the analysis. What was a transcendence above ego, a pure connection with God was transformed into what he thought had to be "evil" based on what he was taught. Not knowing how to articulate that feeling of pure bliss, his conditioning took over, and he now imagined that this "trance" he went into was contact with the devil and he became very afraid. My friend said he never told anyone about this experience until the moment of our conversation. It was the innocence of a child that allowed him to surrender to that silence and disconnect from the illusion of his ego and come into the reality of present moment awareness, connecting with his soul, his own true self. I felt sad for that scared little boy who thought he might have done something wrong. It happened again when he practiced meditation. He said he felt calmer and more focused, but once again, it wouldn't last as he would be challenged by some radical doctrine that put into question his belief in God, and salvation only through religion.

Christ consciousness was described thousands of years before the human man named Jesus even walked among us. It was experienced as pure love, all the divine qualities of the heart: love, joy, compassion, peace, equanimity, tolerance, and acceptance. If you can ask yourself the question, "What would Jesus do?" and operate from that pure love, you're living a Christ conscious life, regardless of your affiliation with a particular organized religion. The moment there is fear of the unknown and different, separation, comparisons, exclusions, judgment, the ego qualities, from what dogma is bred, we lose that divine awareness and no longer live from Christ consciousness. Dr. Deepak Chopra wrote, "All perspectives are valid, yet those that approach nearer to God contain more of the divine qualities, truth, compassion, acceptance and love." Love and compassion breed understanding and provide some breathing space to recognize that all paths lead to God. No one path is better. No one path is superior. Superiority equals separation, and that is fear and ego, not love and oneness, certainly not Christ like.

His Holiness the Dalai Lama, to attendees at the Inter-faith Seminar organized by the International Association for Religious Freedom in Leh, India, on August 25, 2013, addressed the audience, "We must distinguish between belief and respect. Belief refers to total faith, which you must have in your own religion. At the same time, you should have respect for all other religions." Wow, if we, as humans, could only heed this advice. So many wars have been fought in the name of God. I once heard an actress/talk-show host who touts herself as a devout Christian ask a politician, "Are you a man of faith?" The question she was really asking was, "Are you a man of *my* faith?" The truth is we are all striving for the same things. There can be no peace or harmony, no union, no *yoga*, without a level of expanded awareness from every human, particularly when it comes to releasing judgment about someone else's belief systems. And I mean the best parts of those belief systems, the ones steeped in love, rather than those promoted by fear, hatred, oppression, persecution, alienation, and discrimination.

> Love has a power to heal, to reveal divine essence, to restore faith in one's own Being, to bring harmony to all levels of existence —and all these effects lie far beyond feelings. They are tangible results based on spirit. (Dr. Deepak Chopra, *The Path to Love*)

"Attune yourself to Spirit and it will speak to you in love." Do you pray? Do you still love Jesus? Do you believe in God? Many people have shared the same stories of family members becoming defensive and angry as they pursue their own spiritual path. "We discover many truths that only the silent voice of spirit can reveal." Without defending or rationalizing my path, I go inward and trust my own heart. When you need to check in to see if you are on the right track, you need only put your attention on your heart and ask for clarity.

"I love you, and I expect you to behave my way." This has been a contradiction that I've struggled to resolve all my life. Meditation has started to unravel those ties where guilt and self-criticism no longer keep me bound by someone else's views or expectations of me or my relationship to my spirituality. This kind of freedom is called *moksha* in Sanskrit and refers to liberating oneself from the bondage of obligations to others' restrictive ways of thinking, behaving, and living, which often become our own conditioned, automatic, and unconscious ways of thinking, behaving, and living.

Sometimes to others it appears as isolation, but for me, my alone time is a necessary distance to gain clarity of vision in my own life, for my own sense of peace, and to know God's voice through my own expression of love and life. It has little or nothing to do with not wanting to spend time with others, but more to do with spending quality time with myself. The unraveling of layers of conditioning can expose vulnerability so raw that most won't even dare consider it.

I say to you that I know something else to be true—that I believe something differently. (Notice I didn't say the word *different*. I used the word *differently*.) That statement is often interpreted in a particular way, and some people feel it is their job to save someone else's soul. I'm expressing the sameness, the oneness using a slightly different language. You wouldn't challenge the GPS when it takes you on a different route to the same destination. But because I went another way, does that make me unlovable? Does that make me an instant enemy? Shame, manipulation, and guilt are no longer weapons of which I'm afraid.

Jesus voiced a different path to the same destination, and he was crucified. Contradiction, criticism, challenge, and too often, hatred are those unloving qualities, those qualities that come from ignorance and fear. Respect, space, privacy, acceptance, tolerance, nonjudgment through open-mindedness, and introspection are love qualities. Active, fascinating, interesting dialogue transpires when one comes from a heart-centered space toward others, rather than the constricted, unbending, counteroffensive stance.

I refer to my own personal journey, one from being indoctrinated in one particular religion as a child, to the quest, the relentless search, and often being chastised exploration of my own truth. I admire and honor the commitment of those devoted to a particular faith, but I have always questioned, searched, felt unsatisfied, confused, and even afraid, not for me, but for all those who would be damned to hell if they weren't part of the same tribe into which I was born. At the age of seven, I was sent to the principal's office in Catholic school for raising my hand to ask that question. "So all the people unlike me are going to hell? They don't disobey their parents, they don't kill, and they don't lie or steal." My little mind felt confused. And, I remember being really scared, wondering what I had done that was so wrong, except to ask for a bit of clarification on what was being taught in the classroom. No satisfactory answer was ever given. I was just ordered to sit quietly and behave. My questions were deemed an act of misbehaving. That same experience was told to me while living in South Africa decades later when I had similar questions about the rules of a particular religious group. "We don't ask questions." So, you just follow blindly? "If you ask too many questions, you find yourself dead along the back road somewhere" was what the person replied.

I remember seeing the same confusion on *The Oprah Winfrey Show* many years back. A woman from Oprah's audience stood up to talk to a guest, a young, impressionable child, whose parents were members of the Ku Klux Klan. The parents had just given their voice to hateful speech about many different groups of people. The woman began speaking in a kind and gentle tone to the child on stage, who must have been about eight or nine years old. The audience member was developing a rapport with the little girl, asking, "Do you think I seem like a nice lady?" The little girl was guarded, but smiled and said yes. As the conversation between the two continued, it was obvious the child was growing more relaxed. The woman then said, "What if I told you I was Jewish?" Before the child could respond, the parents stood up and began yelling racial slurs at the woman. What was so impactful for me was how neither parent was present enough in that moment to notice how confused and terrified the little girl was because they were so aggressive with their hate speech and party line rhetoric. The child didn't speak again, but the tears rolling down her cheeks were enough to tell the story of how this kind of conditioning instills a deep sense of fear toward anything new, different, or challenging.

How could we be taught God is everywhere and in everything, all loving, all merciful in one lesson and in the next lesson, we were being judged by a big angry man up in the sky and sent to burn in hell?

If God is everyone, everywhere, and in everything, then all of our words, actions, and thoughts, when coming from a pure heart, are divinely guided. That is why yoga became the compass for my life. It made sense to me and resonated in mind, body, and spirit. So much of living a spiritual life is common sense. I started asking questions, but again, much like when I was a young child and kicked out of religion class or kicked out of church, I was met with resistance, annoyance, and anger and often rebutted with fear tactics. This was my experience of being curious. At the same time, I was an avid reader of women's stories. In much of the fiction and nonfiction I read, curious women were either stoned, defiled, deemed crazy, and institutionalized, hidden, or held hostage in the attic or burned at the stake. So, I stopped asking questions of others amid a confusing doctrine and started asking questions of myself.

With these interpretations, it seems ludicrous that the world is at war in the name of God, when we all have the same goal. A terrorist's actions then become a product of basic instinct to reach salvation, while all other options seem unavailable, or so he/she believes at this level of consciousness. Is there any difference between the anger of the opposing sides who are also fighting in the name of God? As Swami Vivekananda suggested back in 1893 to the Parliament of Religion, "If we try to settle our differences by argument or quarreling, we shall find that we can go on for thousands of years without coming to a conclusion. History proves that. The only solution is to march ahead toward the center, toward God, and the sooner we do that, the sooner our differences will vanish."

Mother Meera speaks on this subject saying, "The divine is in the sea. All religions are rivers leading to the sea. Some rivers wind a great deal. Why not go to the sea directly." There was a time in our history, and unfortunately, we see a familiar climate today too, where Mother Meera, rather than be revered for her wisdom, would have been punished for heresy for even suggesting that we could find God on our own.

I remember standing in line at the supermarket in Cape Town, South Africa, and a cashier that I'd become familiar with had donned her scarf in reverence for Ramadan, which had begun earlier in the week. She looked at me, smiling and saying, "Obviously, you are not Muslim." She asked what my religious affiliation was. I told her I grew up Catholic.

It was a moment of true tolerance and impartiality as a Jewish man behind me in line joined the conversation saying, "Are you a practicing Catholic?"

In jest, I replied, "No good Catholic is a practicing Catholic."

Although sacrilegious to some who might read this, they knew I was being ironic, maybe even sarcastic, and we all had a lighthearted moment. The Jesus I have studied over the years taught tolerance, acceptance, nonjudgment, love, and peace. I've struggled all of my life with the discrepancy of what I was told and what seemed to be reality—with motivated interpretations of the religious texts and what was really being said, like how someone could be so pious, extending a hand in peace in the church and within minutes of racing to his car, could be flipping his fellow parishioner a vulgar gesture or spewing one out loud in the parking lot. I am constantly struck with this dichotomy—people who seem very angry, aggressive, intolerant, and sanctimonious toward me, picketing in the streets for the sake of their savior, yet standing with fear and hatred veiling their hearts, with violence in their words, actions, and thoughts. As Deepak Chopra says, "Moral rage is still rage."

I feel compassion and empathy for those beautiful women

who lost their lives in witch hunts for daring to speak their truths, truths that were steeped in love, but seen as heresy because the language was slightly different. My evolution out of a doctrine in which I was inducted wasn't some bold statement against it, but more of a recognition, a remembrance of a truth that was always there beyond the surface of what I was being taught. "You cannot make a plant grow in soil unsuited to it." This statement pertains to so many aspects of life—your passion or purpose, your relationship choices, where you live and work and other choices in life. Vivekananda wrote, "All the various systems of religion, in the end, converge to that one point, that perfect union." With the practices in which I was now engaged, I felt like I could finally exhale. It was as if I finally understood this frustrating quest I was on all of my life. There is no struggle, no challenge, no debate; it's either yum or yuck. It's either love or fear—in all of my words, thoughts, and actions

> Christ was teaching us to aspire to greater heights within ourselves and to even deeper awareness of God's presence within us. Through meditation, contemplation and self-inquiry, we access this as a direct and personal understanding beyond thought. Deep inner experience of the divine has raised them to the realization of God as the only reality in existence. (Swami Kriyananda, *Revelations of Christ*)

Bhakti yoga guides us to accept all points of view as right because the ultimate goal is the same—to reach God and absolute love. When we condemn other points of view of God as "wrong," we cut off the exchange of the exact same energy.

"He who seeks union with it must meditate upon it within the shrine of the heart. It is beyond the grasp of the senses. The intellect cannot understand it. It is out of the reach of thought. Such is Brahman." Adi Shankara in *The Crest-Jewel of Discrimination* was pointing to how words can serve to point us in the direction, but as Dr. Eben Alexander explained after his near-death experience (NDE), that even saying the name God is too small and limiting for the power and awe of the loving presence of our Creator. The moment we try to rationalize or define God, we impose the limitations of our human minds.

> Realization is real religion; all the rest is preparation. Hearing lectures, reading books, or reasoning is merely preparing the ground; it is not religion. Intellectual assent and intellectual dissent are also not religion ... The truths of religion, such as God and Soul cannot be perceived by the external senses.

Swami Vivekananda also speaks to the direct experience, beyond sense perception, reason, and intellect. In the first line in the Tao te Ching, Lao Tzu says the same, "The Tao that can be spoken is not the eternal Tao. The name that can be named is not the eternal name. The nameless is the origin of Heaven and Earth. The named is the mother of myriad things."

Do you think organized religion or our tribal mentality are the biggest culprits for humans remaining asleep, unaware, robotically moving through life in a patriarchal society? Roger Gabriel reminded me that we are all on our own spiritual journeys and someone else's evolution really has nothing to do with your own. Nor, will the timing of those journeys be the same. "We are all on a spiritual journey toward remembering our true nature. We are not here to try and get enlightened. We are enlightened. We just need to remember." He continued, "Some of us have brought memories of God's pure love with us throughout our lives; others devote their lives to God; and others have some traumatic or pivotal experience that jolts them into memory of their divinity."

So how do you reconcile the truth with those who are either

unaware or just immature in their spiritual evolution? I asked Roger's advice on how to live my truth without being castigated from those who might see my path as a threat, or feel it their obligation or responsibility to hijack my soul with their own beliefs. "Stop judging them." I honestly expected Roger to give me some scholarly tips to traverse this bumpy road, but his response proved very profound to me. I am not here to defend my point of view or persuade anyone of anything. We are all on our path; we will take different roads, and we will get there when we get there. Because I truly appreciate his insight, I pushed the issue a bit further with Roger, asking, "I'm not looking to be right. I would just like the same respect I show toward others' beliefs extended to me." And my teacher smiled. "You seem to be under the impression you deserve respect." Most people would not have received that response well, but it actually made me smile as it presented another opportunity for my own spiritual expansion.

He said, "You just have to love them."

When I first met Roger Gabriel, what struck me was that he so matter of fact about meditation while, at the time, I was struggling a bit when challenged by some on the religious right or others who dismissed its value altogether. I asked Roger about what he would you say to my readers about their own resistance to meditation or fears of betraying their faith, or how to respond to those who might challenge them. He said, "Meditation doesn't interfere with religion. Quite the opposite. Meditation strengthens our relationship with God."

Living Yoga

Rather than looking for the differences in other people's spiritual and religious paths, be open to seeing the similarities. Rather than looking to persuade, challenge, force feed your beliefs, take a long deep breath, and remember that each person is doing the best he or she can at the state of their consciousness. Defending your point of view doesn't bring peace. It brings isolation, separation, alienation, and discord. Recognize that someone else's viewpoint isn't wrong or worse. Granting others respect for their views despite the radical difference in yours allows space for God's grace to enter.

Michael A. Singer in *The Untethered Soul* states, "Just as rain makes you wet and fire makes you warm, so you can know the nature of God by looking into the mirror of your transformed self. This is not a philosophy; it is a direct experience." In the movie, *City of Angels*, you clearly see from Dr. Maggie Rice's face how she is experiencing the pear with acute awareness as all of her senses are fired up. The excitement in her eyes as she looks at the particular pear she has chosen—the feel of it in her hand, knowing it's ready to be eaten; the smell of the ripe fruit seeping through the skin; the crisp sound as the flesh of the first bite is separated from the rest of the fruit; and the taste of the sweet juice in her mouth. While the angel Seth can appreciate intellectually that she is enjoying the pear, he cannot relate as he has no idea what a pear smells like, tastes like, etc. He has no direct experience. However, he chooses to descend to earth in physical form, and the movie brings us back to the fruit market where Seth now has a full understanding of Maggie's experience as he tastes a pear for the first time.

No one's interpretation of my personal experience can be taken as the truth of my experience. Even your own direct experience will be your own truth to behold. This is how one develops compassion and loving kindness, by stepping out of one's own belief system to create a space for the other person's experience to exist, to be true for them and respected, regardless of one's own viewpoint, understanding or even acceptance. Intellectually, one might argue for or against my experience or defend one's own perspective, beliefs, cultural systems, or other conditioned responses. Dr. Deepak Chopra wrote, "Yet everyone's mind contains the essence of spirit; silence and intuitive knowledge come naturally to us." This can only be fully known and harnessed when we can create some space, some silence, and stillness in our lives when we relinquish the need to argue and preach or control. Meditation resonates because it navigates the mind away from ego toward spirit and a higher truth.

EIGHT

Is Your Compass Off Kilter?

You will know when your life's compass is oriented properly when you realize you don't have to look for love. You are love. Carl Lentz, the pastor from New York's famed Hillsong Church, says that when you operate from love, your behavior will automatically change. This is what the great sage Patanjali meant when he wrote about spontaneous right action.

So how do you know when your compass is off kilter? There are ways to check in to see if you are out of balance in mind, body, and spirit. Every so often, ask yourself if you are you getting a restful night of sleep or if you are struggling with insomnia or chronic fatigue. Are you including practices in your life that nurture you, along with other members of your family?

When stress goes unchecked and becomes chronic, we can see physical ailments manifest, such as hypertension, heart disease, cortisol overload, and adrenal burnout, along with the elevation or depletion of other hormones.

Living Yoga

- A lack of fulfillment in our lives can make us critical, cynical, and judgmental. Have you been reactive in any or all of these ways? If yes, how can you make improvements to your own attitude?

- Are you accountable for your life and your actions, or do you shift the blame of your misery onto other people, circumstances, or even the household pet? Have you recently said to yourself things like, "It's not my fault. No, I didn't"? Or are you shirking responsibility all together?

- Do you find you are comparing yourself to others with an opinion of superiority or inferiority? Either way, there is a focus on external factors for validation, rather than finding peace and joy from within.

- Are you only focusing on the negative? Would you be willing to develop a habit of saying or thinking, "Thank you," for something or someone in the midst of your misery?

A short time after I moved into a beautiful home in a lovely neighborhood, I discovered that I had rented a home that was built on the toxic waste of an oil company, where hardly any vegetation grew and the entire side of the hill was just a heap of barren, lifeless brownish yellow dirt. The real damage was done back in the 1920s, long before the Environmental Protection Agency existed, and drilling was far less regulated than it is now, but the results of their practices are still evident today. Under better regulations, I guess, oil is still being extracted from the ground. Along the streets throughout this affluent neighborhood are air vents for the wells below which continually expel fumes and keep the gases from setting the whole area aflame.

I've always had a keen sense of smell, so the fumes of petroleum were always apparent to me. Four to six times a year, heavy equipment would be set up outside the front door to do maintenance on the wells. Along with these continuous noxious byproducts of the crude oil, the city also set up gigantic cell towers that stood tall above the community. There was a never-ending buzzing sound that resonated. One day, I realized that my frequent nausea, chronic fatigue, and joint pain were more than likely results of exposure to these toxins that blanketed the environment. We were also adjacent to a local airport, which put us right in the flight pattern of commercial and private aircraft.

I found myself complaining often as I saw a decline in my health, my energy levels, and my overall mood. I was told I was very negative, which, given the living conditions, how could I not be? I thought about my yoga training and decided to focus on all the good things about the house and the neighborhood. It was a safe place to live. The home had a spectacular view and a huge yard in which to host great parties and also raise a polite and happy dog. Each day that I made note of the positive things, I could feel my energy returning a bit more. I also had regular yoga and meditation practices, along with other health regimens. I made certain adjustments to my own environment to alleviate what toxins I could and saw dramatic improvement in my overall wellbeing. A choice to change my attitude from one of "doom and gloom" to gratitude, setting new commitments to deepen my meditation practice, and continuing to examine how I could be more yogic in my daily life shifted not only my perspective, but my reality.

Living Yoga

Take some time to explore your own environment and find ways to bring more pleasant things into your space. Become aware of either how much television you watch or what TV shows you watch. A Reiki healer once suggested I pay attention to my body and the signals it was giving if I watched something unpleasant or violent on television. I was amazed to notice how agitated I felt, how I felt a burning sensation in my stomach, or how easily my mood could be influenced, so I changed what I watched on TV or what movies I agreed to go see.

Are you playing video games? If so, check in and see how your body feels. My mom, who is now eighty-two, became a bit obsessed, like many these days, with certain trending games on her mobile device. Not only was she having trouble sleeping, but her doctor informed her that she had high blood pressure and might have to take medication. She immediately went home and deleted those apps from her phone. Her blood pressure went back to normal! Even little shifts will make a big difference.

> Happiness, we see, is what everyone is seeking; but the majority of us seek it in things that are evanescent and not real. No happiness was ever found in the senses. Happiness is found only in the Spirit. (Swami Vivekananda)

By relating to other people's personal stories throughout the book, maybe you saw similarities in your own circumstances, like the universal themes of fortune and loss. Maybe you began to identify ways in which you might already be living a yogic lifestyle in some ways. I invite you to continue to use the practical exercises in *living yoga* to guide you, to expand and to elevate your consciousness, and to become more aware of your choices. Start asking those questions that lead to deeper meaning. Find stillness within so you can hear the answers. When practicing the principles of yoga, we see how real acceptance, approval, appreciation, and affection are within us. As Marcel Proust said, "The real voyage of discovery consists not in seeking new landscapes, but in having new eyes." Then, you begin to recognize how God becomes a fulfilling experience within oneself, as opposed to an external search or the acceptance of blind faith in something outside of ourselves.

Let your soul and your Spirit guide you. Let love be north on your compass. Meditation, action, knowledge—whichever path resonates most, let that be your center in all aspects of your life. Keep coming back to your center. Reorient your compass to your north, which is the omnipresent, omnipotent, omniscient being that is your soul. And because of the nature of life, we are readjusting all the time and must be easy with ourselves on this journey. Peel back one non-nourishing layer at a time and replace with a layer of nourishment for your life and for your well-being. When you make a commitment to *living yoga*, you realize life excludes nothing, but unifies all in love. If love is your compass, let your heart be the map. As Swami Vivekananda suggests, "Think of your higher self, not of your lower; not of your human misgivings, but your true, divine, glorious nature."

THE RHYTHMS OF NATURE
by Kathleen Nitting

How have we forgotten our soul's purpose?
We are meant to remember to live in harmony with nature.
We are meant to remember we are nature.
We are meant to remember we are part of the infinite
and sacred rhythms of the Divine.

Just like the waves of the ocean meet the shore,
every one of them unique.
Sometimes gliding like a whisper,
other times soaring high with great force.
Never judging, never comparing.
Going with the flow, they merge back into the ocean.

Just as the sun rises and sets without discrimination.
The moon waits patiently in the backdrop for the sun to fade,
never rushing the sun before it reveals its nocturnal glow.
Every so often eclipsing one another reminding us
that when we play superior by standing in someone else's light,
there can only be darkness.

Just like the newborn celebrates its existence,
resting in its pure spirit and trusting life's intelligence to provide.
A baby smiles in remembrance;
and giggles with unbounded joy for still knowing the truth

Just as the animal charges forward in the great migration.
It leaves behind the old and familiar,
forging ahead toward the new and unknown.
With or without fear, it plunges into uncertainty,
continuing with an innate trust, a deeper sense of knowing

There's no mystery.
Sometimes it gets messy, other times, pristine.
Sometimes the cupboards are bare,
other times, you just find 100 bucks on the street.
Sometimes the wildebeest gets caught in the crocodile's jaws,
other times, it leaps onward to the river bank.
Sometimes there's a victory,
other times, pain in the defeat.
There's no mystery...
the only path is one of acceptance and gratitude
for having conquered the experience,
allowing the current to guide and propel you forward.

Just like the palm tree surrenders to the gusts,
bending and swaying with the flow,
accepting, never judging the wind.
Our journey to freedom is in the bending,
in the swaying, in the merging with all that is.
That's living in the rhythms of nature.

I am in gratitude ... in love ... in yoga.

End

References

AUTOBIOGRAPHY OF A YOGI, Paramahansa Yogananda
Copyright 1946, ISBN-13-978-0-87612-079-8, 13TH Edition, 1998
International Publications Council of Self-Realization Fellowship

SHANKARA CREST-JEWEL OF DISCRIMINATION: Timeless Teachings of Non-Duality
Adi Shankara, Translated by Swami Prabhavananda and Christopher Isherwood
ISBN-13 978-0-87481-038-7, 1947, 1975
Vedanta Society of Southern California, Vedanta Press

THE YOGA SUTRAS OF PATANJALI
Translated an Introduced by Alistair Shearer
ISBN-0-609-60959-9
Bell Tower, 1982

PATHWAYS TO JOY: The Four Paths to God, Swami Vivekananda
Edited by Dave Deluca
ISBN-978-1-930-722-67-5
New World Library, 2003

THE SEVEN SPIRITUAL LAWS OF YOGA: A Practical Guide to Healing Body, Mind, and Spirit
Deepak Chopra, M.D. and David Simon, M.D.
ISBN-13-978-0-471-73627-1
John Wiley & Sons, 2004

THE PATH TO LOVE: Spiritual Strategies for Healing, Deepak Chopra, M.D.
ISBN-0-609-80135-X
Three Rivers Press, 1997

THE THIRD JESUS: The Christ We Cannot Ignore, Deepak Chopra, M.D.
ISBN-978-0-307-33832-7
Three Rivers Press, 2008

FREE TO LOVE, FREE TO HEAL: Heal Your Body by Healing Your Emotions, David Simon, M.D.
ISBN-978-0-9819640-1-0
Chopra Center Press, 2009

THE UPANISHADS, Introduced and translated by Eknath Easwaran
ISBN-978-1-58638-021-2
The Blue Mountain Center of Meditation, Nilgiri Press, 1987, 2007

THE BHAGAVAD GITA, Introduced and translated by Eknath Easwaran
ISBN-978-1-58638-019-9
Nilgiri Press, 1985, 2007

THE DHAMMAPADA, Introduced and translated by Eknath Easwaran
ISBN-978-1-58638-020-5
Nilgiri Press, 1985, 2007

LIVING BUDDHA, LIVING CHRIST, Thich Nhat Hanh
ISBN-1-57322-018-3
Riverhead Books, The Penguin Group, 1995, 2007

THE CLOUD OF UNKNOWING, Anonymous

EMOTIONAL INTELLIGENCE: Why it can Matter More than I.Q., Daniel Goleman
ISBN-978-553-38371-3
Bantam Books, 1997

THE UNTETHERED SOUL: The Journey Beyond Yourself, Michael A. Singer
ISBN-13-978-1-57224-537-2
New Harbinger Publications, 2007

THE BOOK OF AWAKENING: Having the Life you Want by Being Present to the Life you Have, Mark Nepo
ISBN-978-1-57324-117-5
Conari Press, 2011

SEVEN THOUSAND WAYS TO LISTEN: Staying Close to What is Sacred, Mark Nepo
ISBN-978-1-4516-7468-2
Atria Paperback, 2012

THE WAR OF ART: Break Through the Blocks and Win Your Inner Creative Battles, Steven Pressfield
ISBN-978-1-936891-02-3
Black Irish Entertainment, 2002

HEARTSONGS, Mattie J.T. Stepanek
ISBN-0-7868-6947-X
Hyperion Books, 2001, 2002

A NEW EARTH: Awakening to Your Life's Purpose, Eckhart Tolle
ISBN-978-0-452-28996-3
Plume, The Penguin Group, 2006

THE POWER OF NOW: A Guide to Spiritual Enlightenment, Eckhart Tolle
ISBN-978-1-57731-480-6
New World Library and Namaste Publishing, 1999, 2004

THE BIBLE, KJV

Bhakti Yoga - The Path of Love by Roger Gabriel

The Eight Limbs, the Core of Yoga by William J.D. Doran

CPSIA information can be obtained
at www.ICGtesting.com
Printed in the USA
FSHW04n0503040418
46461FS